Best of Fons&Porter

QUILT LOVER'S Gifts

FONS & PORTER STAFF
Editors-in-Chief Marianne Fons and Liz Porter

Editor Jean Nolte
Assistant Editor Diane Tomlinson
Managing Editor Debra Finan
Technical Writer Kristine Peterson

Art Director Tony Jacobson
Graphic Designer Emily Sheeder

Editorial Assistant Mandy Couture
Sewing Specialist Cindy Hathaway

Contributing Photographers Craig Anderson, Dean Tanner, Katie Downey
Contributing Photo Assistant DeElda Wittmack

Publisher Kristi Loeffelholz
Advertising Manager Cristy Adamski
Retail Manager Sharon Hart
Web Site Manager Phillip Zacharias
Customer Service Manager Tiffiny Bond
Fons & Porter Staff Megan Franck, Peggy Garner, Shelle Goodwin, Kimberly Romero, Laura Saner, Karol Skeffington, Yvonne Smith, Natalie Wakeman, Anne Welker, Karla Wesselmann

New Track Media LLC
President and CEO Stephen J. Kent
Chief Financial Officer Mark F. Arnett
President, Book Publishing W. Budge Wallis
Vice President, Publishing Director Joel P. Toner
Vice President, Group Publisher Tina Battock
Vice President, E-Commerce Dennis O'Brien
Vice President, Circulation Nicole McGuire
Vice President, Production Derek W. Corson
Production Manager Dominic M. Taormina
Production Coordinator Kristin N. Burke
IT Manager Denise Donnarumma
Renewal and Billing Manager Nekeya Dancy
Online Subscriptions Manager Jodi Lee

Our Mission Statement
Our goal is for you to enjoy making quilts as much as we do.

LEISURE ARTS STAFF
Vice President and Editor-in-Chief Susan White Sullivan
Quilt and Craft Publications Director Cheryl Johnson
Special Projects Director Susan Frantz Wiles
Senior Prepress Director Mark Hawkins
Imaging Technician Stephanie Johnson
Prepress Technician Janie Marie Wright
Publishing Systems Administrator Becky Riddle
Mac Information Technology Specialist Robert Young

President and Chief Executive Officer Rick Barton
Vice President of Sales Mike Behar
Director of Finance and Administration Laticia Mull Dittrich
National Sales Director Martha Adams
Creative Services Chaska Lucas
Information Technology Director Hermine Linz
Controller Francis Caple
Vice President, Operations Jim Dittrich
Retail Customer Service Manager Stan Raynor
Print Production Manager Fred F. Pruss

Library of Congress Control Number: 2011943966
ISBN-13/EAN: 978-1-60900-375-3
UPC: 0-28906-05615-0

We're thrilled to bring you this collection of some of our very favorite gift ideas! The projects we've included are among our most popular of all time. You'll find patterns for lots of quick and easy items for everyone on your gift list. Enjoy the beautiful photography as you browse through the pages to find the project that's just right for you. Whether you want to make a little quilt, pillows, or sewing accessories, you'll find plenty to love. You'll also appreciate our trademarked *Sew Easy* lessons that will guide you via step-by-step photography through any project-specific special techniques. We think you'll have fun stitching these gifts for your family and friends!

Happy quilting,

Marianne + Liz

Table of Contents

8

37

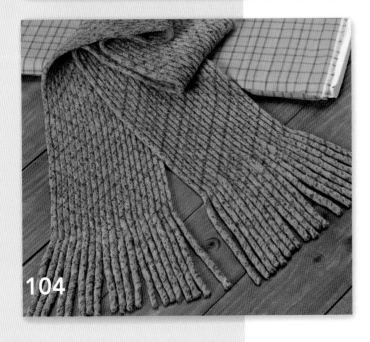

104

25 Quick Gifts	6
Partridge in a Pear Tree	8
Cutting Mat Bag	12
Take-Along Work Surface	14
Ruler Holders	16
Easy Quilt Rack	19
Trapunto: Dove Pincushion	20
Wool Sewing Wallet	23
Rabbit Pinkeeper	28
Wool Neck Purse	31
Wool Needlecase	34
Button Box	37
Itty Bitty Penny Rug	40
Centennial Basket	42
Prairie Cabin Mini	46
Go Fish	48
Kuku Bird	52
Springy Flowers	55
Tulip Mini	60
This Flower is for You	64
Ginger's Flower Garden	68
Primitive Checkerboard	72
Quillow	78
Yo-Yo Basket Pillow	82
My Style Pillows	87
Gift Card Pockets	92
Gift Bags	96
Quilted Purse and Accessories	98
Crazy About Quilts Watchband	102
Chenille Scarf	104
Fleece Baby Blanket	107
Dolly Bag	108

Coloring Apron 111

Groovy Backpack 114

Wrap It to Go 117

Buttons & Bows 120

Pillowcases 123

Flannel Brick Road 124

Friends Forever 127

My Little House 132

Rickrack Runner 134

Coiled Fabric Bowls 136

Love Note 139

Be Mine 143

Cathedral Window Ornaments 148

English Basket Ornament 150

Holly Days Table Runner 152

Yo-Man & Yo-Landa 156

50 Secret Sister Gifts 159

Shopping for Your Favorite Quilter 160

Techniques

Sew Easy: Decorative Embroidery
Stitches 25

Sew Easy: Bead Embellishments 54

Sew Easy: Yarn Binding 58

Sew Easy: Making Yo-Yos 84

Sew Easy: Faux Chenille 106

Sew Easy: Cutting Half-Square Triangles 131

Sew Easy: Basic Beading 142

Sew Easy: English Paper Piecing 151

General Instructions 164

114

136

127

1) Give a "quilt in a jar." Collect all the fabrics for a paper-pieced miniature quilt, package them in a jar, and give them to a quilting friend (Instructions available at www.CarolDoak.com). **2)** Knock someone's socks off by creating a *Yo-Yo Basket Pillow* (see page 82 for instructions). **3)** Make or

25 Quick Gifts

13) Buy a packet of fancy hot drink mix and give it with a pretty mug. **14)** Give a journal to a quilter so she can keep a record of her quilts. **15)** Make a beautiful wall quilt (see page 60 for instructions). **16)** Sew a handy Cutting Mat Bag (see page 12 for instructions). **17)** Give a pair of warm, fuzzy slippers or socks a friend can wear while

purchase some notecards with quilt designs on them. **4)** Give a gift certificate for her favorite quilt shop or spa. **5)** Give a spool or two of neutral 100% cotton thread for piecing. **6)** Make or buy a cute pincushion for your quilt friend's sewing room. **7)** Give a disposable camera for taking photos at the next quilt show.

8) Buy a copy of one of the latest quilting books. **9)** Create an *Itty Bitty Penny Rug* (see page 40 for instructions), frame it, and give it. **10)** Give a punch needle embroidery kit, or, complete a project such as *My Little House* on page 132. **11)** Whip up *Flannel Brick Road* for the guy on your list (see page 124 for instructions). **12)** Use a leftover quilt block to make a toss pillow for the sofa.

Here's a collection of gift ideas that quilters can buy or make for friends and family members!

quilting on a cold night. **18)** Delight a young lady with *Buttons & Bows* (see page 120 for instructions). **19)** Make a pillowcase to give as a gift. **20)** Create a snow couple (see page 156). **21)** Wrap up a pretty thimble. **22)** Make a quilter a wool sewing wallet (see page 23 for instructions). **23)** Give a pair of embroidery scissors. **24)** Send your quilting buddy a chatelaine. **25)** Fold up some fat quarters and tie them with a ribbon.

QUILT BY **Kim Schaefer**. MACHINE QUILTED BY **Diane Minkley**.

Partridge
IN A PEAR TREE

Add this wallhanging to your holiday decor this year.
Don't be surprised if your family breaks into song when they see it!

PROJECT RATING: EASY
Size: 51" × 59"

MATERIALS

NOTE: Fabrics in the quilt shown are from the Partridge in a Pear Tree collection by Kim Schaefer for Andover Fabrics.

¾ yard brown print for background

1 fat quarter★★ black print for border corners

7 dark print fat eighths★—1 black, 1 brown, 2 red, and 3 green

5 assorted light print fat quarters★★ in tan and cream

3 fat eighths★ assorted gold prints

⅞ yard black print for inner border and binding

1½ yards border print for outer border

Paper-backed fusible web

Black embroidery floss (optional)

3½ yards backing fabric

Twin-size quilt batting

★fat eighth = 9" × 20"

★★fat quarter = 18" × 20"

Cutting

Measurements include ¼" seam allowances. Border strips are exact length needed. You may want to make them longer to allow for piecing variations. Patterns for appliqué are on page 11. Follow manufacturer's instructions for using fusible web.

From brown print, cut:
• 1 (20½" × 28½") rectangle for center background.

From black print fat quarter, cut:
• 2 (6"-wide) strips. From strips, cut 4 (6") C squares.

From each dark print fat eighth, cut:
• 1 (4½"-wide) strip. From strip, cut 4 (4½") A squares.

From remainder of 1 red print fat eighth, cut:
• 1 Heart.

> ### Sew **Smart**™
> Apply fusible web to remainder of brown print fat eighth before cutting Tree Trunk and Branches.
> —Marianne

From remainder of brown print fat eighth, cut:
• 1 (½" × 17") rectangle for Tree Trunk.
• 1 (¼" × 16") rectangle for Bottom Tree Branch.
• 1 (¼" × 12") rectangle for Middle Tree Branch.
• 1 (¼" × 10") rectangle for Top Tree Branch.

From remainder of green print fat eighths, cut a total of:
• 46 Leaves.

From each light print fat quarter, cut:
• 3 (2½"-wide) strips. From strips, cut 12 (2½" × 4½") B rectangles.

From remainder of light print fat quarters, cut:
• 1 Partridge.
• 1 Wing.
• 1 Pot.
• 1 Large Pot Band.
• 1 Small Pot Band.

From each gold print fat eighth, cut:
• 2 (2½"-wide) strips. From strips, cut 7 (2½" × 4½") B rectangles.
• 4 Pears.
• 1 Beak from 1 print only.

From black print, cut:
• 4 (2½"-wide) strips. From strips, cut 2 (2½" × 36½") side border #2 and 2 (2½" × 32½") top and bottom border #2.
• 7 (2¼"-wide) strips for binding.

From border print, cut:
• 4 (6"-wide) **lengthwise** strips, centering design. From strips, cut 2 (6" × 48½") side border #4 and 2 (6" × 40½") top and bottom border #4.

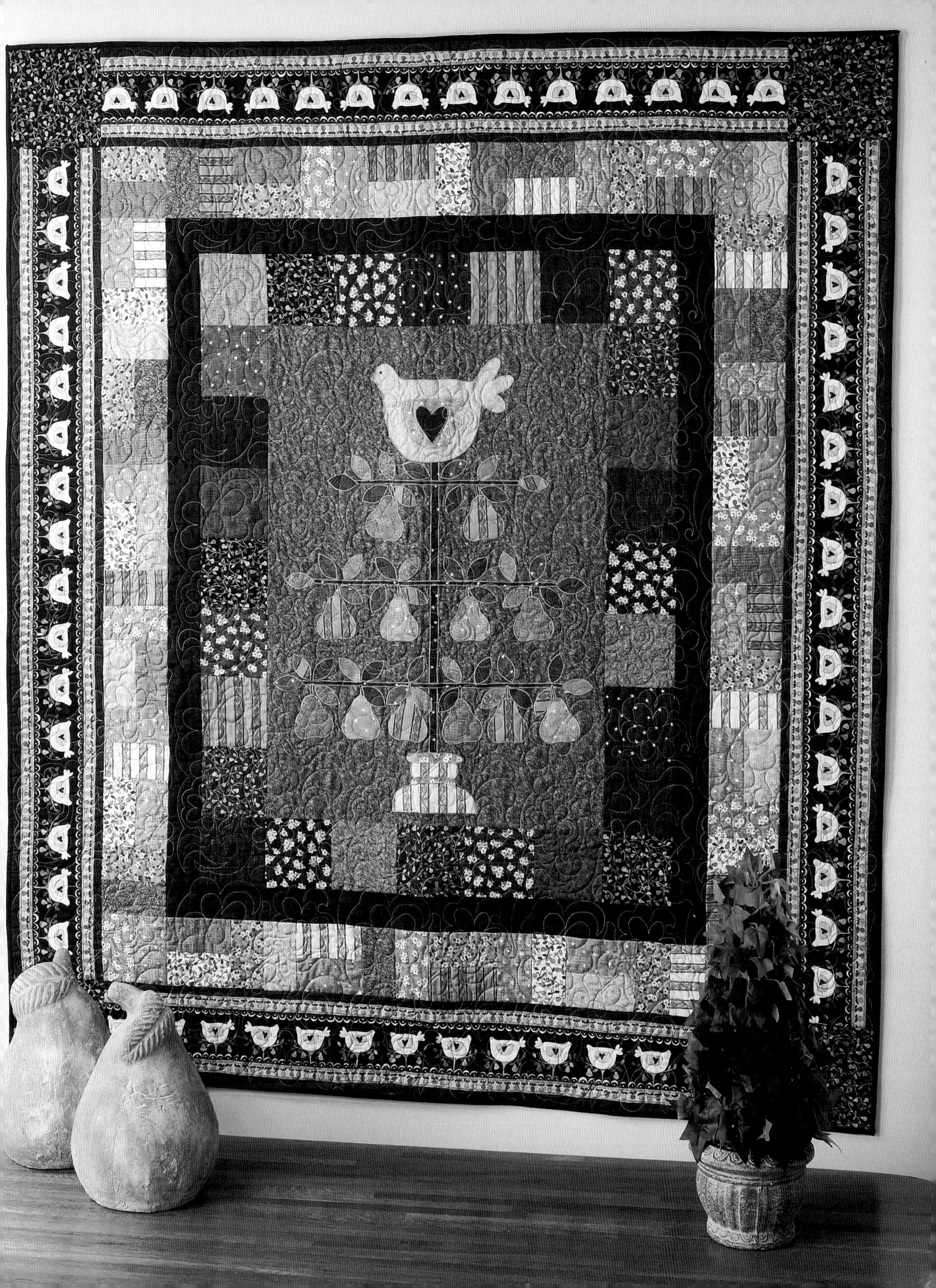

Quilt Center Assembly

1. Referring to photo on page 9, arrange appliqué pieces on brown print center background rectangle; fuse in place.

2. Machine appliqué around pieces, using a short, narrow zigzag stitch and tan thread.

3. Draw eye on partridge with fine-point permanent marker or embroider eye using black floss and satin stitch.

Quilt Assembly

1. Join 7 dark print A squares as shown in *Quilt Top Assembly Diagram* to make 1 border #1. Make 4 border #1.

2. Add 1 border #1 to each side of quilt center. Add remaining borders to top and bottom of quilt.

3. Add 1 black print side border #2 to each side of quilt. Add top and bottom border #2 to quilt.

4. Join 2 assorted B rectangles as shown in *Border Unit Diagrams*. Make 40 Border Units.

Border Unit Diagrams

5. Referring to *Quilt Top Assembly Diagram*, join 10 Border Units to make 1 border #3. Make 4 Border #3.

6. Add 1 border #3 to each side of quilt. Add remaining borders to top and bottom of quilt.

7. Add 1 side border #4 to each side of quilt. Add 1 black print C square

to each end of top and bottom border #4. Add borders to quilt.

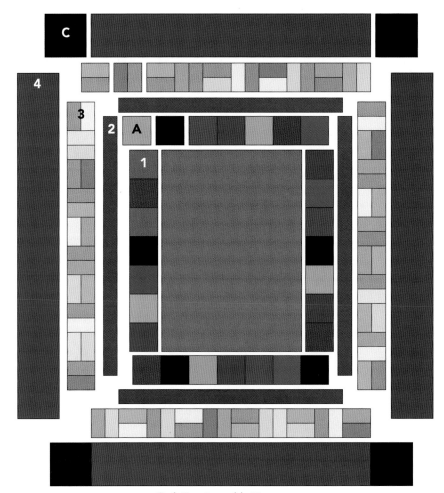

Quilt Top Assembly Diagram

Finishing

1. Divide backing into 2 (1¾-yard) lengths. Join panels lengthwise. Seam will run horizontally.

2. Layer backing, batting, and quilt top; baste. Quilt as desired. Quilt shown was quilted with an allover floral design *(Quilting Diagram)*.

3. Join 2¼"-wide black print strips into 1 continuous piece for straight-grain French-fold binding. Add binding to quilt.

Quilting Diagram

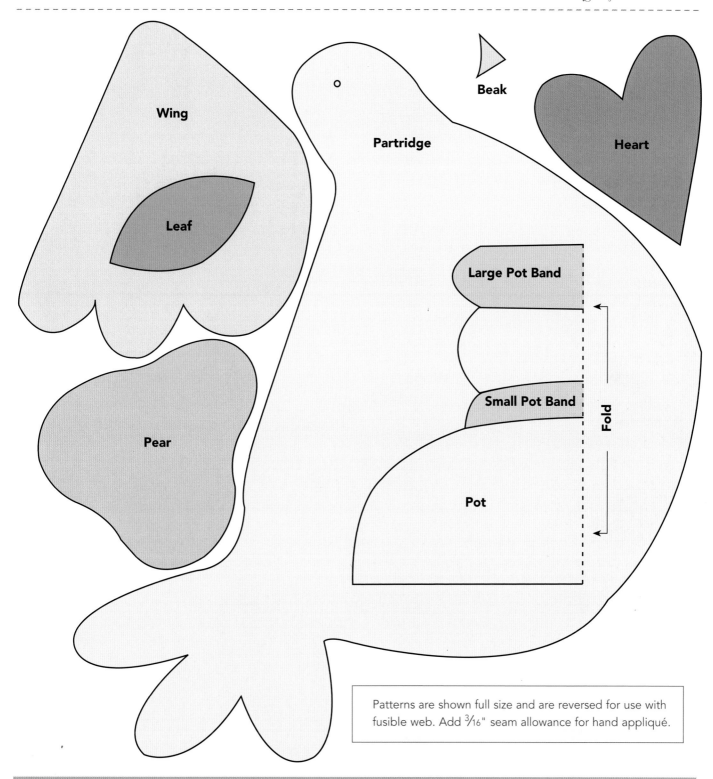

Wing

Leaf

Pear

Partridge

Beak

Heart

Large Pot Band

Small Pot Band

Fold

Pot

Patterns are shown full size and are reversed for use with fusible web. Add ³/₁₆" seam allowance for hand appliqué.

DESIGNER

Kim Schaefer is a pattern designer and owner of Little Quilt Company. She also designs fabric for Andover Fabrics. Look for Kim's book, *Quilts, Bibs, Blankies, Oh My*, published by C&T Publishing, at your local quilt shop. ✳

PROJECT BY **Jean Nolte**.

Cutting Mat Bag

This great bag is just the right size to tote your 18" × 24"
cutting mat and 24"-long rulers to your next quilt workshop. The exterior pockets
easily accommodate a rotary cutter and other supplies.

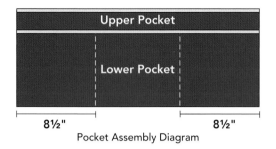

Pocket Assembly Diagram

Upper Pocket

Lower Pocket

8½"   8½"

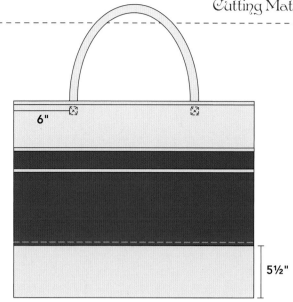

6"

5½"

Assembly Diagram

PROJECT RATING: EASY

Size: 26" × 20½"

MATERIALS

NOTE: Fabrics in the quilt shown are from the Up in Stitches collection by Fabri-Quilt.

2 yards double-sided prequilted fabric

⅜ yard tan stripe for binding

Size 16/100 Denim or Sharp sewing machine needles

1" piece of hook and loop tape

Walking foot or even-feed presser foot (optional)

Cutting

Measurements include ½" seam allowances. Zigzag or serge close to edges of all pieces to prevent seam allowances from fraying as you handle fabrics. Reinforce all seams by stitching a second time, ⅛" from first seam.

From prequilted fabric, cut:

• 1 (4"-wide) **lengthwise** strip. From strip, cut 2 (4" × 30") rectangles for straps.

From remaining prequilted fabric, cut:

• 2 (21½"-wide) strips. From strips, cut 2 (21½" × 27") rectangles for bag front and back.

• 1 (10½"-wide) strip. From strip, cut 1 (10½" × 27") rectangle for upper pocket.

• 1 (8½"-wide) strip. From strip, cut 1 (8½" × 27") rectangle for lower pocket.

From tan stripe, cut:

• 4 (2¼"-wide) strips for binding. Join strips into 1 continuous piece for straight-grain French-fold binding.

Bag Assembly

1. Fold 1 strap rectangle in half lengthwise with wrong sides facing; press fold to mark handle center. Bring long raw edges into center with wrong sides facing and press. Fold strap in half so raw edges are concealed. Topstitch close to edges of strap and lengthwise through center of strap. Repeat to make second strap.

2. Add binding to top edge of upper pocket. Repeat for lower pocket.

3. Press under ½" on bottom of lower pocket. Referring to *Pocket Assembly Diagram*, place lower pocket atop upper pocket, right sides up, tucking bottom edge of upper pocket into folded edge of lower pocket. Baste folded edge of pocket section.

4. Topstitch through both layers of pocket section to divide lower pocket into 3 sections as shown.

5. Place pocket section atop bag front as shown in *Assembly Diagram*. Topstitch lower edge of pocket section to bag front.

6. Stitch hook and loop tape to inside of upper pocket section and bag front.

7. Place bag front atop bag back, right sides facing; stitch along sides and bottom edges. Turn right side out, press.

8. Add binding to top edge of bag.

9. Position 1 handle on inside front of bag as shown. Topstitch through all layers to attach handle to bag. Repeat for bag back. ✳

TAKE-ALONG
Work Surface

Peggy Schafer designed this handy cutting and pressing mat to help solve the
problem of working in a confined area at home or at a quilt class.

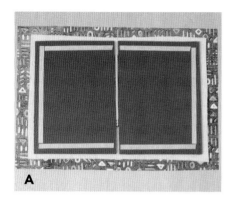

A

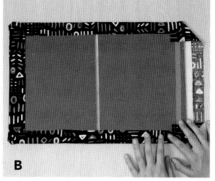

B

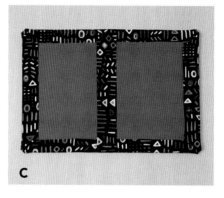

C

PROJECT RATING: EASY

Size: 9½" × 12½"

MATERIALS

1 Omnimat® 12WG (8¾" × 11¾")
   cutting mat

½ yard fabric for cover

13" × 19" rectangle of cotton or
   cotton blend batting

2 (9" × 12") rectangles (¼"-thick)
   hardboard or plywood

8½" × 11" piece felt

Steam-A-Seam2® ½"-wide fusible
   tape

Paper-backed fusible web

1¼"-wide double-sided carpet tape

Pencil

Cutting

Follow manufacturer's instructions
for using fusible web.

From cover fabric, cut:
- 1 (15" × 22") rectangle.
- 1 (2" × 13") rectangle.

Assembly

1. Referring to *Photo A*, place large
rectangle of fabric right side down
on table. Center batting on fabric.

2. Center hardboard rectangles
side by side over batting, rough
sides down. Place pencil between
boards and slide boards snugly
against it.

3. Place Steam-A-Seam2® strips on
hardboard, sticky side down, ½" in
from top, bottom, and outer side
edges as shown in *Photo A*. Press
in place with your fingers.

4. Remove paper from Steam-A-
Seam2® strips. Referring to *Photo
B*, pull corners of fabric over board
and finger press in place. (Add
additional short strips of Steam-A-
Seam2® if needed to secure fabric.)
Pull top edge of fabric over strips
and secure. Repeat with bottom
edge and then each side. Remove
skewer or pencil.

5. Fold under ½" on narrow ends of
small rectangle; press. Place Steam-

A-Seam2® strips on wrong side
of fabric along both long sides of
rectangle. Remove liner paper.
Referring to *Photo C,* center
rectangle over gap between 2
hardboard pieces. Finger press in
place.

6. Following manufacturer's
instructions, fuse all areas where
Steam-A-Seam2® strips were used.

7. Cover back side of felt with
fusible web. Peel off backing paper
and fuse felt to left hardboard
piece (see photo on page 14).
Make sure fabric edges are covered
by felt. Place 3 strips of double-
sided carpet tape on back side
of cutting mat. Affix mat to
remaining hardboard piece.

Sew **Smart**™

**Turn your entire work surface
over to make a mini ironing board
for class. —Liz** ✳

Ruler Holders

These hanging caddies, with pockets in a variety of sizes,
will help you organize all your quilting rulers and tools.

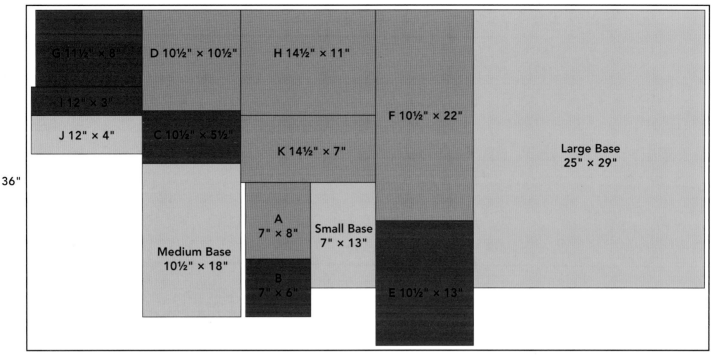

Ruler Holder Cutting Diagram

PROJECT RATING: EASY
Ruler Holder Sizes:
Small: 7" × 11"
Medium: 10½" × 16"
Large: 25" × 27"

MATERIALS

NOTE: Materials listed are for 3 ruler holders.

2¼ yards (36"-wide) red fiberglass screen

1¼ yards print for binding

⅝"-diameter rods or dowels for hanging (optional)

Cutting

Refer to *Ruler Holder Cutting Diagram* to cut pieces from fiberglass screen.

From print, cut:

• 16 (2¼"-wide) strips for binding.

Small Ruler Holder Assembly

1. Bind top edges of A and B rectangles with straight-grain French-fold binding.

Sew **Smart**™
Attach binding to back of piece, fold over to front, and topstitch in place. —Marianne

2. Referring to *Small Ruler Holder Diagram*, place A and B rectangles atop small base rectangle, right sides up, aligning bottom edges. Baste in place.

3. Bind outer edges of ruler holder.

4. Fold 2" of top edge of ruler holder to front. Topstitch in place to form pocket for rod.

Small Ruler Holder Diagram

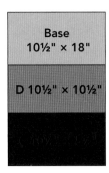

Base
10½" × 18"

D 10½" × 10½"

Medium Ruler Holder Diagram

Medium Ruler Holder Assembly

1. Bind top edges of C and D rectangles.

2. Referring to *Medium Ruler Holder Diagram*, place C and D rectangles atop medium base rectangle, right sides up, aligning bottom edges. Baste in place.

3. Bind outer edges of ruler holder.

4. Fold 2" of top edge of ruler holder to front. Topstitch in place to form pocket for rod.

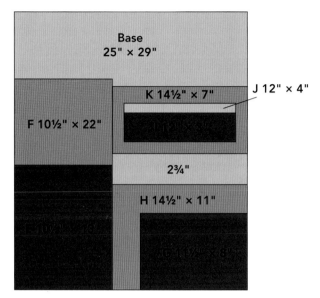

Base
25" × 29"

K 14½" × 7"

J 12" × 4"

F 10½" × 22"

2¾"

H 14½" × 11"

Large Ruler Holder Diagram

Large Ruler Holder Assembly

1. Bind top edges of E, F, H, I and J rectangles.

2. Bind top and left side of G rectangle.

3. Bind top and bottom of K rectangle.

4. Referring to *Large Ruler Holder Diagram*, place E rectangle atop F rectangle, right sides up, aligning bottom edges. Baste in place. Bind right side of E–F Unit.

5. Place G rectangle atop H rectangle aligning bottom and right edges. Baste in place. Topstitch left side of G rectangle to make pocket.

6. Place I rectangle atop J rectangle aligning bottom edges. Baste in place. Bind sides and bottom of I–J Unit.

7. Center I–J Unit atop K rectangle. Topstitch sides and bottom of I–J Unit to make pocket.

8. Place E–F Unit atop large base rectangle, aligning bottom and left side. Place G–H Unit atop base, aligning bottom and right side. Place I–J–K Unit atop base 2¾"

from top of G–H Unit, aligning right side. Baste all units in place. Right side of binding on E–F Unit should overlap left side of G–H and I–J–K units.

9. Topstitch along both edges of binding between E–F and G–H and I–J–K units.

10. Bind outer edges of ruler holder.

11. Fold 2" of top edge of ruler holder to front. Topstitch in place along both sides of binding to form pocket for rod.

DESIGNER

Teresa Sue Carmine learned to sew on her grandmother's treadle sewing machine when she was just six years old. She enjoys sewing, weaving, and beading. ✳

Easy Quilt Rack

PROJECT RATING: EASY

Size: A 24" shelf kit will accommodate a quilt 16"–20" wide.

MATERIALS

NOTE: Shelf kits are available in several sizes, finishes, and styles. Some stores offer brackets and shelves separately. Choose a shelf that is 4"–6" longer than the quilt you want to display.

Shelf kit that includes:
    24" shelf
    2 brackets
    Screws and drywall fasteners
Set of (2) wooden closet pole cups
Hammer and small nail
¾" × 24" dowel rod
Acrylic varnish (2 oz. bottle)
Foam brush
Screwdriver
Small ruled square (6") and tape
    measure or yardstick
Wood glue
Small saw
2 (¾"-long) wood screws (optional)
Level (optional)

Display your latest quilt—plus a few knickknacks—on a stylish and adaptable quilt rack you can easily make yourself from materials purchased at a home improvement store.

> **Sew Smart™**
> If you like, purchase an unfinished shelf or kit and paint it to match your room decor. —Marianne

Assembly

1. Using acrylic varnish and foam brush, seal the wood of closet pole cups and dowel rod. (The acid pH of raw wood can damage fabric.)

2. Using ruled square, measure and mark inside edges of wooden brackets to position closet pole cups. Position cups so they will be the same distance from the top and back of the bracket. Position the cups near the back of the brackets if you want the quilt to hang close to the wall. For a larger folded quilt, attach the cups closer to the center.

3. Use hammer and small nail to make small pilot "starter" holes so screws will go in easier.

4. Attach cups. If screws included with cups are too long for brackets, substitute shorter ones.

5. Using hardware included in shelf kit, attach brackets to wall, spacing them so the distance between closet pole cups equals the width of the quilt plus about ¾". A level is handy for making sure you

position the brackets at the same height. You can also measure down from the ceiling.

6. Measure distance inside closet pole cups to determine correct length for dowel. Use saw to cut dowel approximately ⅛" shorter. Insert dowel in cups.

7. Center shelf atop brackets. If your rack is located where it could be bumped, secure shelf to brackets by squeezing a thin line of wood glue on top of each bracket.

8. Hang your quilt and enjoy!

> **Sew Smart™**
> You can also use a pre-assembled shelf if exact fit isn't important.
> —Liz ✳

Quilt shown is from Quilter's Complete Guide by Fons & Porter.

PROJECT BY **Faith Reynolds**.

TRAPUNTO:
Dove Pincushion

Stitch this adorable trapunto pincushion or ornament entirely
on your embroidery machine. You can download the digitized design from our
Web site at www.FonsandPorter.com/dovedesign.

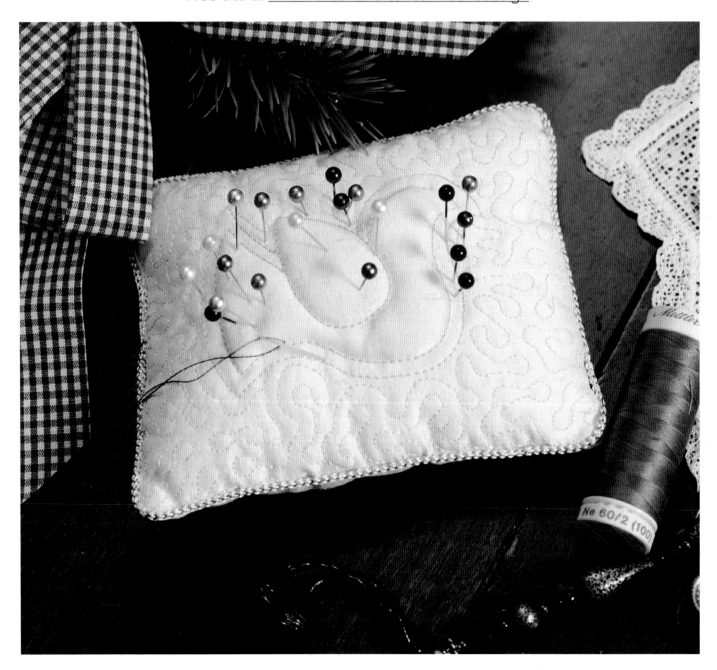

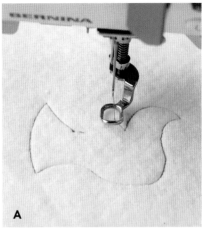

A

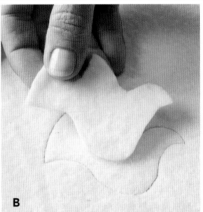

B

C

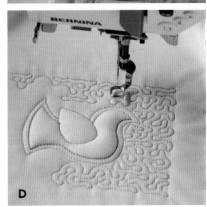

D

PROJECT RATING: EASY

Size: 4½" × 3⅞"

MATERIALS

2 (9" × 14") rectangles of cream solid fabric (We used dupioni silk for an elegant look.)

1 (9" × 14") rectangle of muslin for lining

2 (9" × 14") pieces of low loft quilt batting

Embroidery machine or module

Spray temporary adhesive for paper patterns

Spray temporary fabric adhesive

Gold polyester embroidery thread

Polyester fiberfill

¾ yard gold decorative piping (optional)

Clear monofilament nylon or polyester thread

Edgestitch presser foot for sewing machine (optional)

Embroidery Machine Method

1. Place batting atop wrong side of muslin. Hoop with batting side up. Embroider first "color," creating an outline of dove design *(Photo A)*. Remove hoop from machine. **Do not remove fabric from hoop at this time.**

2. Trace dove design on page 22 onto paper. Cut out pattern. Spray back of pattern with temporary adhesive for paper patterns.

3. Fold remaining batting piece in half. Place pattern atop batting and cut out dove shape. You will have 2 pieces of dove-shaped batting.

4. Spray batting dove shapes with temporary fabric adhesive. Place batting dove shapes atop batting in hoop within stitched dove outline *(Photo B)*.

5. Spray hooped batting with temporary fabric adhesive. Place top layer of fabric right side up on top of batting layer *(Photo C)*. Finger press firmly in place.

6. Attach hoop to embroidery module. Using embroidery thread, embroider next "color." Stitching will outline dove and stipple background around dove. The extra batting creates the trapunto effect for dove *(Photo D)*.

7. Remove hoop from embroidery module, but don't remove fabric from hoop. Spray right side of outer edges of backing fabric with spray temporary fabric adhesive. Place right sides together over embroidery in hoop. Finger press firmly in place.

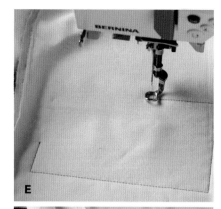

E

F

G

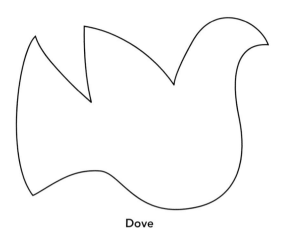

Dove

8. Stitch last "color" which is the straight stitch outline of pincushion *(Photo E)*. Remove hoop from module and fabric from hoop.

9. Trim excess fabric from outer edges, leaving ¼" seam allowance on all sides *(Photo F)*. Trim corners. Turn pincushion right side out through opening.

10. If desired, attach cord trim around pincushion either by hand or with sewing machine. To attach cord trim with a sewing machine, use an edgestitch presser foot and thread machine with clear monofilament thread. Begin stitching at opening for turning. Place blade of foot between decorative cord and pincushion edge. Select a narrow zigzag stitch and adjust stitch width so "zig" sews into edge of fabric and "zag" catches edge of cord. At end, overlap ends of cord and tuck them into opening.

11. Stuff the pincushion lightly *(Photo G)*. Hand stitch opening closed.

DESIGNER

Faith Reynolds is an educator specializing in embroidery and embroidery software. She regularly teaches and has written magazine articles, on-line sewing classes, and educational materials. ✳

WOOL Sewing Wallet

Take-along stitching has never been more popular. Make yourself one of these little sewing kits to keep your tools and threads together in your purse. They are also great gifts for friends who often sew in waiting rooms or at ballgames.

PROJECT RATING: EASY
Size: 4¼" × 9"

MATERIALS

2 (4¼" × 9") pieces of coordinating felted wool for wallet exterior and interior

Small scraps (about 3½" square) of contrasting colors of felted wool for trims

2 (½"–¾"-diameter) buttons

6" black elastic cord

Assorted seed beads

Quilting thread or other strong thread for attaching beads

Assorted colors of embroidery floss or perle cotton

Freezer paper for templates

Cutting

Using patterns on page 24, trace hearts, flower, leaves, and butterfly onto freezer paper and cut out shapes. Press shiny side of freezer paper templates to wool and cut around each piece.

From wool scraps, cut the following pieces for wallet interior:

• 2 (1½") squares for small pockets. Round off lower corners as shown in *Interior Diagram*.

• 1 (1½" × 2") rectangle for Needle Keeper.

• 1 Large Heart.

• 1 Small Heart.

• 1 (2") square for Seam Ripper Holder.

• 1 (2½" × 3½") rectangle for large pocket. Round off corner slightly.

From wool scraps, cut pieces for flower, leaves, and butterfly for wallet exterior.

Wallet Interior Assembly

NOTE: See *Sew Easy: Decorative Embroidery Stitches* on pages 25–27 for instructions for all stitches used in this project. If desired, add lettering or embroidery to small pieces before stitching them to wallet.

1. Referring to *Interior Diagram*, center and blanket stitch 1 small pocket to large pocket. Add beads to each upper pocket corner.

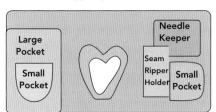

Interior Diagram

2. Pin large pocket to lower left corner of wallet interior; blanket stitch pocket to interior along right edge of pocket. Blanket stitch along top edge of pocket without stitching to wallet. Baste or pin lower and left pocket edges to wallet interior.

3. Center and blanket stitch Small Heart on Large Heart. Blanket stitch Large Heart to center third of wallet interior, stitching sides to wallet. Top curve and bottom center of heart should be blanket stitched without stitching through the wallet piece, creating a scissors pocket that is open at top and bottom.

4. Pin remaining curved pocket to lower right corner of wallet interior and blanket stitch around sides and bottom. Along top edge of pocket, blanket stitch through pocket only.

5. Cross stitch 1½" × 2" needle keeper piece to top right corner.

6. Blanket stitch along 2 opposite sides of 2"-square Seam Ripper Holder. Fold square in half, bringing raw edges together. Treating raw edges as one, blanket stitch raw edges to right third of wallet interior.

Wallet Exterior Assembly

1. Fold wallet exterior piece in thirds and press to create positioning guidelines.

2. Blanket stitch leaves, flower, and butterfly to left third of wallet exterior. Add beads as desired.

3. Stitch one button at each spot indicated with an X on *Exterior Diagram*.

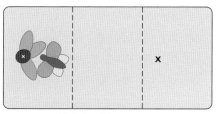

Exterior Diagram

4. Fold cord elastic in half and tie ends in an overhand knot. Loop elastic around button on right edge.

Wallet Assembly

1. Pin wallet exterior and interior pieces together with wrong sides facing.

2. Round off corners of wallet rectangles.

3. Beginning at top left edge of interior large pocket, blanket stitch around wallet to join pieces together.

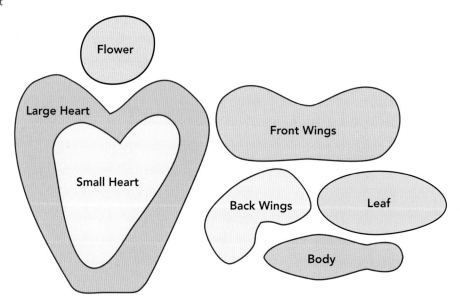

DESIGNER

Rachel Wells has been quilting for more than twenty years. She finds great satisfaction in having twelve to fifteen quilts in various stages of completion at any given time. She lives in Missoula, MT. ✳

Sew *Easy*™ Decorative Embroidery Stitches

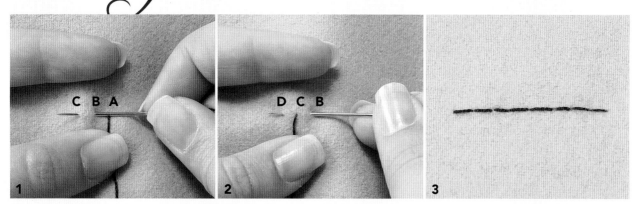

Backstitch: 1. Bring needle to right side of fabric at A. Insert needle at B and bring it up at C. Pull thread until stitch lies flat. **2.** Insert needle at B and bring it up at D. (First stitch is hidden by needle.) **3.** Continue stitching in this manner. Secure thread on back side by making a shallow knot.

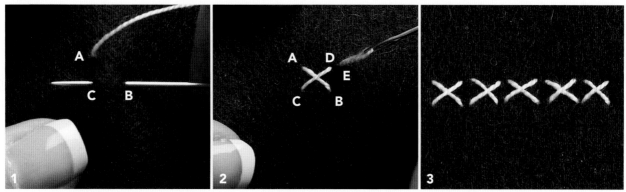

Cross Stitch: 1. Bring needle to right side of fabric at A. Insert needle at B and bring it up at C. Pull thread until stitch lies flat. **2.** Insert needle at D and bring it up at E. **3.** Continue in this manner. Secure thread on back side by making a shallow knot.

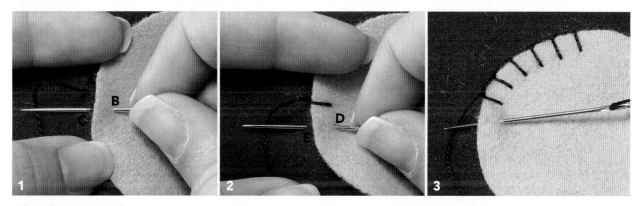

Blanket Stitch: 1. Bring needle to right side of fabric at A, just outside the edge of the appliqué piece. Insert needle at B and bring it up at C, over the thread. Pull thread taut so stitch lies flat, but not tight enough to pucker fabric. **2.** Insert needle at D and bring it up at E, over the thread. **3.** Continue in this manner. Secure last stitch with a tiny stitch to anchor the loop.

Sew Easy™ Decorative Embroidery Stitches

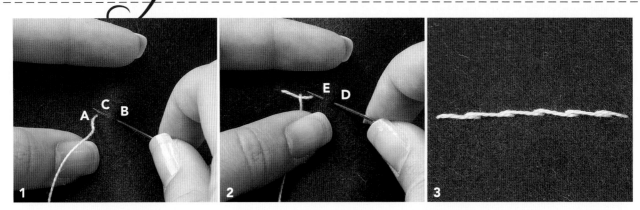

Stem Stitch: **1.** Bring needle to right side of fabric at A. Insert needle at B and bring it up at C. **2.** Insert needle at D and bring it up at E. **3.** Continue in this manner. Secure thread on back side by making a shallow knot.

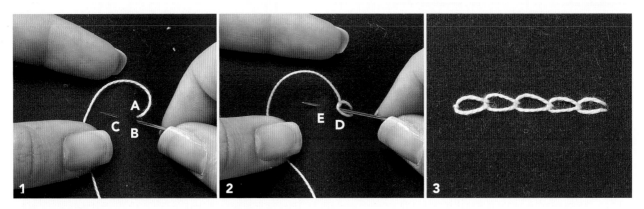

Chain Stitch: **1.** Bring needle to right side of fabric at A. Insert needle at B and bring it up at C, over the thread. Pull thread, creating a loop. **2.** Insert needle at D inside the loop. Bring needle up at E, over the thread. Pull thread, creating a loop. **3.** Continue in this manner. Secure last stitch with a tiny stitch to anchor the loop.

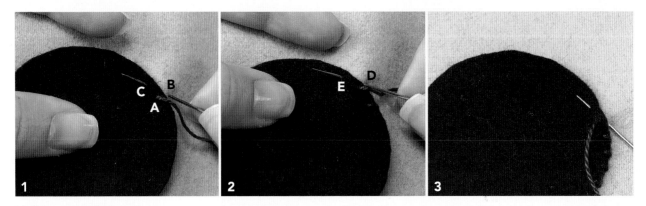

Whipstitch: **1.** Bring needle to right side of fabric at A, through background and appliqué piece. Insert needle at B, just outside the edge of the appliqué piece. Bring needle to right side at C through background and appliqué piece. **2.** Insert needle at D and bring it up at E. **3.** Continue in this manner. Secure thread on back side by making a shallow knot.

Sew Easy™ Decorative Embroidery Stitches

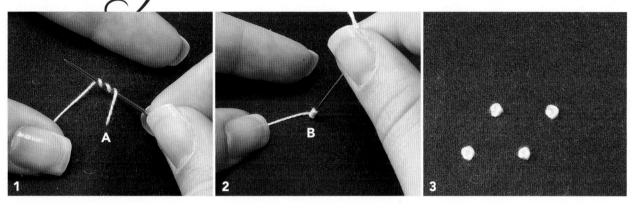

French Knot: 1. Bring needle to right side of fabric at A. Wrap thread around needle 2 or 3 times, keeping needle near the fabric surface. **2.** Insert needle at B, right beside A. Holding the thread to keep loops wrapped around needle, gently pull thread through the loops to form a knot. **3.** Repeat to make desired number of French knots. Secure thread on back side by making a shallow knot.

Spoke Stitch: 1. Bring needle to right side of fabric at A. Insert needle at B and bring it up at C. Pull thread until stitch lies flat, but not tight enough to pucker fabric. **2.** Insert needle at D and bring it up at E. **3.** Insert needle at F and bring it up at G. **4.** Insert needle at H. Secure thread on back side by making a shallow knot.

Sew Smart™

If the wool you have chosen tends to ravel or fray, try felting it. Start with pieces larger than needed for design since wool will shrink considerably when machine washed and dried. Wool designated as "washable wool" will not felt. If you are working with recycled clothing scraps or other "mystery" wool, it may or may not felt.

FELTING WOOL 1. Set washing machine for a small load and hot wash, cold rinse cycle. **2.** Sort wool pieces into light and dark groupings. (Dyes used to color wool have a tendency to bleed when wet, so group fabric pieces accordingly.) Place smaller wool pieces in a mesh bag designed for washing lingerie. **3.** Machine wash wool; dry in dryer at hot setting.

PROJECT BY **Sue Spargo**.

Rabbit Pinkeeper

Stitch this pinkeeper for yourself or as the perfect gift for a friend. It's "sew" much fun, you'll want to make more than one of these charming little treasures!

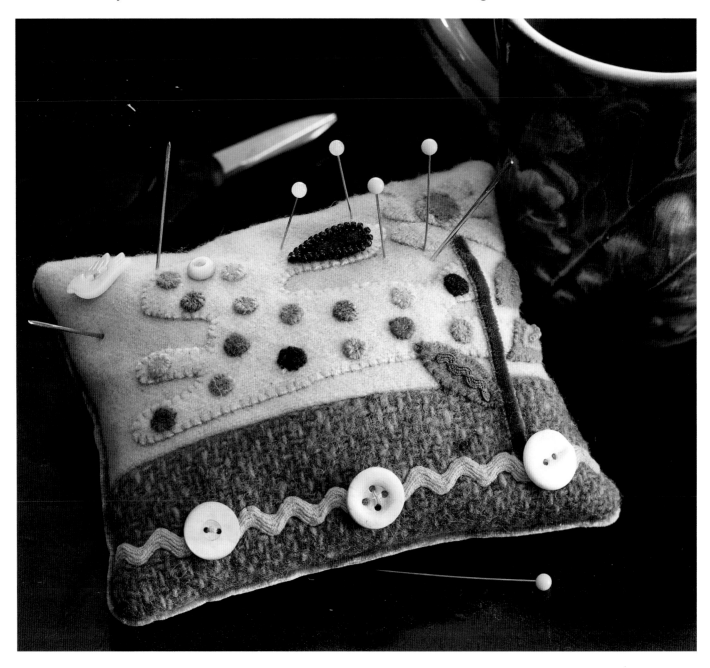

PROJECT RATING: EASY

Size: 5½" × 4½"

MATERIALS

6" squares assorted wool felt in light
green and blue for background

6" square pale pink wool felt for
rabbit

Scraps of wool felt in aqua, green,
orange, blue, pink, rose and teal
for appliqué

6" square rose velveteen for back

1 fat eighth★ tightly woven cotton
for lining

3 (½"-diameter) white buttons

1 (¼"-diameter) button for
rabbit eye

1 white bird button

Scraps of turquoise and green
rickrack, turquoise chenille yarn,
and green velvet ribbon

Green and rose seed beads

Freezer paper

¼" hole punch (optional)

Fons & Porter Glue stick (optional)

Polyester fiberfill or sand

Lavender buds (optional)

★fat eighth = 9" × 20"

Cutting

Measurements include ¼" seam
allowances. Make freezer paper
patterns for appliqué shapes on
page 30. Press freezer paper patterns
onto wool. Cut shapes from desired
fabrics; remove paper.

> **Sew Smart™**
>
> If your wool is thin or ravels
> easily, iron fusible web on the
> wrong side as a stabilizer. —Liz

From light green wool, cut:
• 1 (5½" × 3½") rectangle.

From blue wool, cut:
• 1 (5½" × 2") rectangle.

From pale pink wool, cut:
• 1 Rabbit.

From rose wool, cut:
• 1 Inner Ear.

From turquoise wool, cut:
• 1 Flower.

From green wool, cut:
• 3 Leaves.

From assorted wool scraps, cut:
• 1 Flower Center.
• 16 (¼"-diameter) circles.

> **Sew Smart™**
>
> Use a ¼" hole punch to punch the
> small dots. —Sue

From rose velveteen, cut:
• 1 (6" × 5") rectangle for pinkeeper
back.

From lining fabric, cut:
• 2 (6" × 5") rectangles.

Assembly

1. Join light green and blue rectangles
as shown in *Assembly Diagrams* to
make pinkeeper top background.

2. Baste 1 lining rectangle to wrong
side of pinkeeper top background
and 1 lining rectangle to wrong
side of pinkeeper back.

3. Referring to photo and *Assembly
Diagrams*, arrange appliqué pieces,
velvet ribbon stem, and rickrack
on pieced background rectangle.

> **Sew Smart™**
>
> A dot of glue will hold appliqué
> pieces until you sew them in
> place. —Marianne

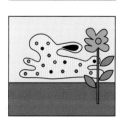

Assembly Diagrams

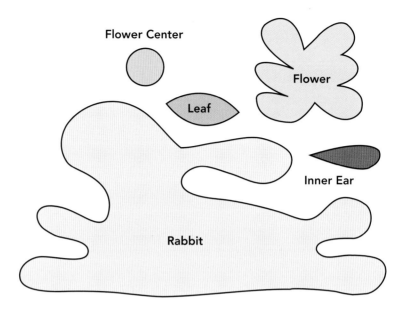

Couching Diagram

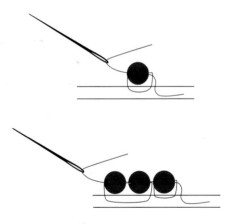

Beading Diagrams

4. Using matching thread, whipstitch pieces to background. Blanket stitch around rabbit and dots using matching thread *(Blanket Stitch Diagram* on page 25*).*

5. Couch turquoise yarn around flower center *(Couching Diagram).* Add green beads to leaf and rose beads around inner ear *(Beading Diagrams).* Attach buttons as shown in photo..

6. Place pinkeeper top atop pinkeeper back rectangle, right sides facing. Stitch around all sides with a ¼" seam, leaving an opening in the bottom seam for turning.

7. Turn pinkeeper right side out. Stuff with fiberfill or sand. Whipstitch opening closed.

Sew **Smart**™
Add ½ cup of lavender buds for a great fragrance. —Sue

DESIGNER

Sue Spargo's creative appliqué projects have been influenced by the energy and color of traditional African designs and her love of primitive arts and crafts. With her sister, she creates the Earthworks range of hand-dyed wool. ✳

WOOL Neck Purse

Tuck your embroidery scissors, thimble,
and thread into this charming neck purse to keep
them handy when stitching.

PROJECT RATING: EASY
Size: 5" × 6¼"

MATERIALS

7" × 16" piece black wool for purse
7" × 16" piece cotton fabric for
  lining
5" square medium blue wool for
  basket
3" × 4" piece gold wool for star and
  flowers
3" × 4" piece red wool for flowers
  and cord covers
1 yard black cording for neck strap
2 (1") squares hook and loop tape
  fasteners
Black, gold, and green perle cotton
  or embroidery floss
White glue

Cutting

Appliqué patterns are on page 33.

From black wool, cut:

- 1 (5½" × 6½") rectangle for purse
  front.
- 1 (5½" × 8") rectangle for purse
  back.

From cotton fabric, cut:

- 1 (5½" × 7") rectangle for lining
  front.
- 1 (5½" × 8½") rectangle for lining
  back.

From blue wool, cut:

- 1 basket.

From gold wool, cut:

- 1 star.
- 9 flowers.

From red wool, cut:

- 2 (1") squares for cording covers.
- 9 flowers.

Assembly

Refer to photos on page 31 and
below for placement of appliqué
pieces. Stitch diagrams are shown on
pages 25–27.

1. Position star on basket and
  blanket stitch with gold thread.

2. Center basket on purse front,
  with bottom of basket ½" above
  bottom edge of purse front.
  Blanket stitch with black thread.

3. Position flowers on purse front,
  leaving 1½" at the top edge empty
  so flap won't cover appliqués.

4. Attach each flower by stitching
  from the center to the outside,
  making 6–8 "spokes." Use gold
  thread on gold flowers and black
  thread on red flowers. Stitch a
  French knot in center of each
  flower, using green thread for gold
  flowers and gold for red flowers.

5. Using green thread, stem stitch
  stems and a vine to connect
  flowers. With gold thread, make
  a few French knots between the
  flowers.

6. Lay purse front atop purse back,
  right sides together, with bottom
  edges even. Machine stitch around
  sides and bottom with ¼" seam.
  Turn right side out.

7. Make flap by turning top edge of
  purse back to purse front. Mark
  fold line with a pin. Lay out 1 red
  and 2 gold flowers on flap. Attach

flowers with "spoke" stitch; add stem stitch vine and French knots as shown in photo.

8. Lay lining front atop lining back, right sides together, with bottom edges even. Stitch around sides and bottom with ¼" seam. Do not turn right side out. Place lining into purse. Fold under ¼" along front edge and flap of lining and pin to purse. Blanket stitch lining to purse around flap and front of purse using black thread.

9. Cut cording to desired length. Apply white glue to ends to prevent raveling. Fold 1 red wool square in half; place end of cording into fold and stitch through wool and cording to secure. Place wool piece on top side edge of purse and blanket stitch to purse using black thread. Repeat for other end of cord.

10. Position a square of hook and loop tape at each end of flap; sew 1 half to underside of flap and other half to front of purse.

DESIGNER

Pat Sloan is a nationally-known quilt designer and teacher who specializes in folk-art appliqué.

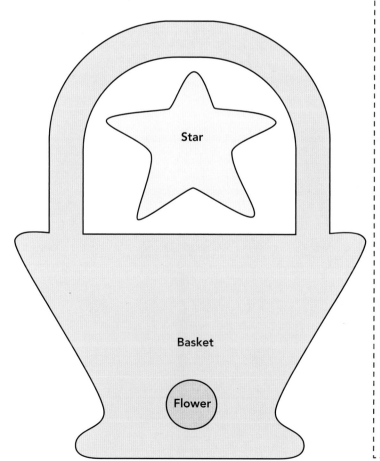

Star

Basket

Flower

TRIED & TRUE

Marianne Fons used the basket and flower motifs to make a table rug in light shades of wool. ❋

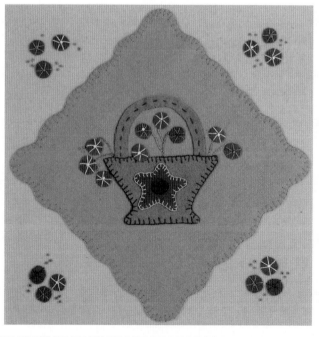

PROJECT BY **Marjorie Berry Hansen**.

WOOL Needlecase

Just a few scraps of wool or felt are needed to make this cute needlecase. It's the perfect gift for your best quilting friend.

PROJECT RATING: INTERMEDIATE

Size: 4¾" × 3¼"

MATERIALS

¼ yard dark green wool or felt

4" square red wool or felt

4" square light green wool or felt

Gold and light green pearl cotton

1 snap set

Cutting

Patterns are on page 36.

From dark green wool, cut:

• 2 Background/Lining pieces.

• 2 Handles.

• 1 Needle Keeper.

From red wool, cut:

• 1 Star.

• 4 Flowers.

From light green wool, cut:

• 1 Stem.

• 1 Stem reversed.

• 8 Leaves.

Needlecase Assembly

1. Referring to photo on page 34 and *Needlecase Assembly Diagram*, arrange appliqué pieces on dark green background piece.

2. Using gold thread, blanket stitch star to background. (See *Blanket Stitch Diagram* on page 25.) Using light green thread, attach stems with "X" stitch, and leaves with slip stitch. Using gold thread, stitch a French knot in the center of each flower to attach to background (*French Knot Diagram* on page 27).

3. Stitch needle keeper to lining piece along stitching line as shown in *Needlecase Interior Diagram*. Attach snap pieces to lining where indicated by circles.

4. Fold each handle in half lengthwise. Whipstitch edges together. Pin handle to wrong side of background piece as shown in *Needlecase Assembly Diagram*.

5. Lay appliquéd background piece atop lining piece, wrong sides together, with handles sandwiched between them. Using gold thread, blanket stitch through both layers around outer edge, catching handles in stitching.

6. Block needlecase (except handles) on a flat surface covered with a towel. Place a wet cloth atop needlecase and press. Let piece dry before moving.

Needlecase Assembly Diagram

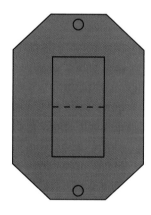

Needlecase Interior Diagram

DESIGNER

Marjorie Berry Hansen is a quilter, craftsperson, and designer from Johnston, Iowa. She enjoys working in wool felt. ✳

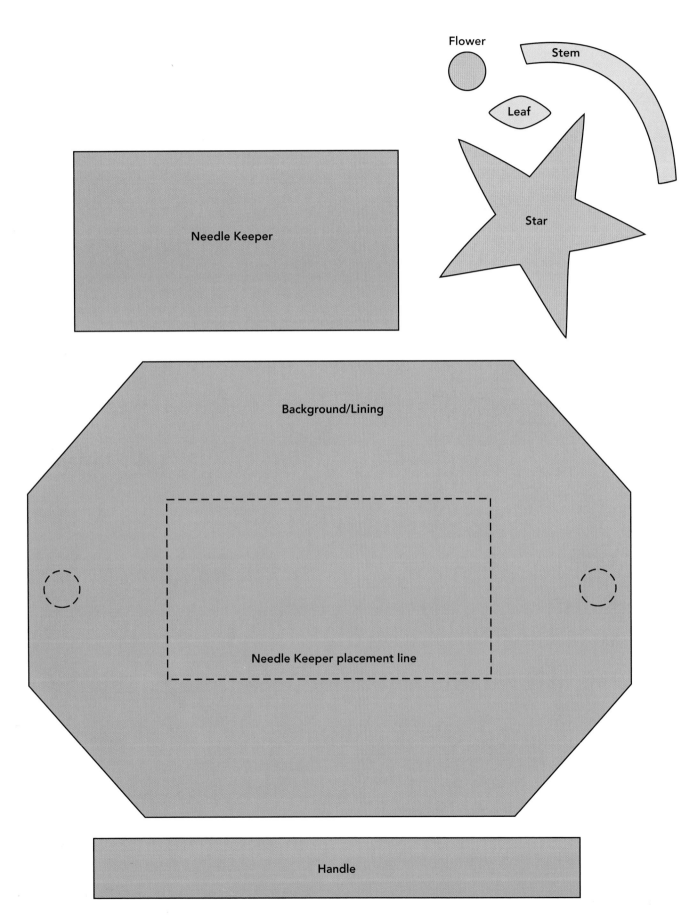

Flower

Stem

Leaf

Needle Keeper

Star

Background/Lining

Needle Keeper placement line

Handle

Button Box

Designer Julie Larsen used wool appliqué to cover this button box. Make one to hold an antique button collection or to use as a gift box for a special present.

PROJECT RATING: EASY

Size: 8"-diameter

Assembly Diagram

MATERIALS

¼ yard tan wool or felt

4" square dark red wool or felt

5" square bright red wool or felt

7" square green wool or felt

Red, green, and gold embroidery
floss

Red pearl cotton

8"-diameter craft box

Freezer paper

Glue stick

5 small gold beads (optional)

Black paint (optional)

Cutting

Patterns for appliqué pieces are
below. Cut templates from freezer
paper. Trace box lid for circle
template. Lightly press freezer paper
templates to wool, cut out shapes,
and peel off freezer paper.

From tan wool or felt, cut:

• 1 Circle.

• 1 (¾" × 26") strip.

From dark red wool or felt, cut:

• 1 Large Flower.

From bright red wool or felt, cut:

• 1 Large Flower.

• 1 Small Flower.

From green wool or felt, cut:

• 3 Leaves.

• 1 (¼" × 7") strip for long stem.

• 1 Short Stem.

Assembly

1. Referring to *Assembly Diagram*,
position long stem strip on tan
felt circle. Glue in place with glue
stick. Using 1 strand of green
embroidery floss, whipstitch stem
in place.

2. Position remaining felt appliqué
pieces on tan felt circle and
whipstitch in place, using 1 strand
of matching embroidery floss.

3. Using 3 strands of green
embroidery floss and a running
stitch, stitch a vein in each leaf.

4. Using 3 strands of gold embroidery
floss, stitch French knots in center
of large flower *(French Knot
Diagram* on page 27*)*. Add gold
beads if desired.

5. Glue tan felt strip to edge of
lid, overlapping ends. Trim extra
length.

6. Place appliquéd tan felt circle atop
box lid. Tack in place with dots

of glue. Using tan thread, closely
whipstitch circle to tan strip.
This stitching should be almost
invisible.

7. Blanket stitch around edge
of circle with red pearl cotton
(Blanket Stitch Diagram on page
25*)*.

8. Paint box if desired.

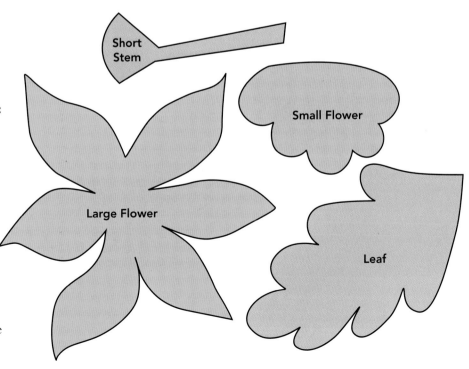

TRIED & TRUE

Make a 16" square pillow.

MATERIALS

10" square dark red wool or felt
5" square bright red wool or felt
7" square green wool or felt
1 fat quarter cream plaid homespun
¼ yard red and green plaid
    homespun
Red, green, and gold embroidery
    floss
Red pearl cotton
16" square pillow form

Cutting

From dark red wool or felt, cut:
• 1 Large Flower.
• 4 (½" × 10") strips.

From bright red wool or felt, cut:
• 1 Large Flower.
• 1 Small Flower.

From green wool or felt, cut:
• 3 Leaves.
• 1 (¼" × 7") strip for long stem.
• 1 Short Stem.

From cream plaid homespun, cut:
• 1 (10") square

**From red and green plaid
homespun, cut:**
• 1 (16½") square for pillow back.
• 2 (3¾" × 16½") strips.
• 2 (3¾" × 10") strips.

Assembly

1. Appliqué flowers and leaves on cream homespun square as described in button box instructions.

2. Baste dark red wool felt strips to sides of cream square, aligning outer edges. Baste remaining dark red strips to top and bottom edges of square in same manner.

3. Add side borders to pillow center. Add top and bottom borders.

4. Place pillow top and back right sides facing. Sew around edge, leaving a 3" space for turning. Turn right side out. Stuff pillow and slipstitch opening closed.

DESIGNER

Julie Larsen enjoys using innovative methods to create traditional quilts. She is the owner of Prairie Star Quilts in Elk Horn, Iowa. Contact her at: Prairie Star Quilts, 4132 Main Street, Elk Horn, Iowa 51531, (712) 764-7012, www.prairiestarquilts.com ✳

Itty Bitty Penny Rug

Use your tiniest scraps of wool to make this adorable primitive. Finish it in a small frame to display with other folk art items on a table or shelf.

PROJECT RATING: EASY
Size: 5" × 7"

MATERIALS

3" square each of purple, pink, blue, gold, brown, brown tweed, beige, and green wool
5" × 7" rectangle black wool
5" × 6" rectangle blue plaid wool
7" × 9" rectangle tan stripe flannel
Quilting, sewing, or embroidery threads to match wools
Freezer paper
5" × 7" picture frame

Cutting

Patterns for appliqué shapes are on page 41. Trace patterns on dull side of freezer paper. Rough cut around shapes. Press to adhere paper shapes to wool. Cut wool shapes on traced lines. Leave paper on wool until ready to stitch.

> ### Sew **Smart**™
> If your wool is thin or ravels easily, iron fusible web on the wrong side as a stabilizer.
> —Marianne

From purple wool, cut:
• 7 Berries.
From pink wool, cut:
• 1 Tulip.
From blue wool, cut:
• 1 Bird.
From green wool, cut:
• 10 Leaves.
From gold wool, cut:
• 2 Windows.

From brown wool, cut:
• 1 Door.
From beige wool, cut:
• 1 House.
From brown tweed wool, cut:
• 1 Roof.
From blue plaid wool, cut:
• 2 Long Borders.
• 2 Short Borders.

Assembly Diagram

DESIGNER

Bonnie Sullivan is addicted to textiles! Her love of fabric and quilting was handed down to her through generations of quilters, but especially by her mother. Bonnie has been designing penny rug patterns since 2000, and currently designs fabric for Maywood Studio. ✳

Assembly

NOTE: See *Sew Easy: Decorative Embroidery Stitches* on pages 25–27 for instructions for all stitches used in this project.

1. Cut a 3" × 5" piece of freezer paper. Iron to center of 5" × 7" black rectangle. Using contrasting thread, baste around freezer paper close to the edge. Remove paper.

2. Referring to *Assembly Diagram*, arrange all pieces except borders on black rectangle inside basted line. Whipstitch pieces in place using matching thread.

3. Using green thread, outline stitch stems. Using beige thread, straight stitch lines on windows. Using gold thread, stitch a French knot for doorknob.

4. Baste borders to black rectangle, aligning straight edges with basting line. Borders will overlap slightly at corners. Whipstitch borders in place. Remove basting thread.

5. Referring to photo, carefully trim away excess black background, leaving a generous ⅛" outside borders.

6. Center design on tan stripe flannel rectangle and whipstitch in place using black thread.

7. Frame in 5" × 7" frame.

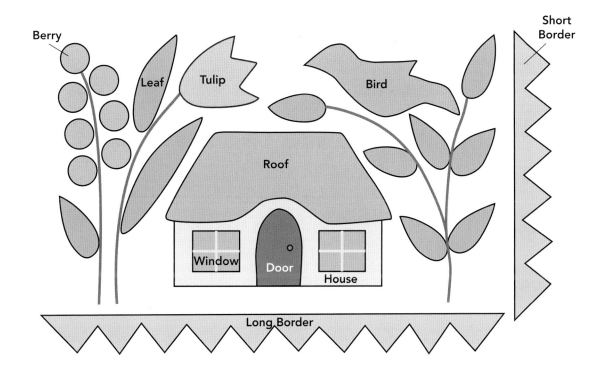

Centennial Baskets

This charming basket by designer Judie Rothermel combines patchwork and appliqué. Frame it as she did or add traditional binding for a small wallhanging.

PROJECT RATING: INTERMEDIATE

Size: 9" × 9"

Block: 1 (4½") Basket block

MATERIALS

10" square tan print for background

8" square dark gold print for basket and flower centers

6" square light gold print for basket

4" square each of medium blue print #1 and red print for flower petals

6" square dark blue print for stems and leaves

6" × 11" rectangle medium blue print #2 for corner triangles

Paper-backed fusible web

9" square backing fabric

9" square quilt batting

9"-square picture frame (optional)

masking tape (optional)

Cutting

Patterns for appliqué pieces are on page 45. Measurements include ¼" seam allowances. Follow manufacturer's instructions if using fusible web.

From tan print, cut:

• 1 (6⅛") square. Cut square in half diagonally to make 2 half-square E triangles (1 is extra). Referring to *Cutting Diagrams*, place 5" line of ruler along 1 short side of E triangle and trim off tip. Repeat for other short side of E triangle to make top background piece.

• 2 (1⅛" × 3⅜") C rectangles.

• 1 (2⅛") square. Cut square in half diagonally to make 2 half-square D triangles (1 is extra).

From dark gold print, cut:

• 6 (1½") squares. Cut squares in half diagonally to make 12 half-square A triangles (1 is extra).

• 2 Handles.

• 3 Centers.

From light gold print, cut:

• 3 (1½") squares. Cut squares in half diagonally to make 6 half-square A triangles (1 is extra).

• 1 (1⅛") B square.

From each of medium blue print #1 and red print, cut:

• 3 Petals.

From dark blue print, cut:

• 1 Center Stem.

• 1 Side Stem.

• 1 Side Stem reversed.

• 2 Large Leaves.

• 4 Small Leaves.

From medium blue print #2, cut:

• 2 (5") squares. Cut squares in half diagonally to make 4 half-square F triangles. Triangles are over-sized.

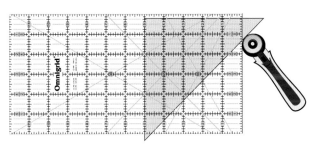
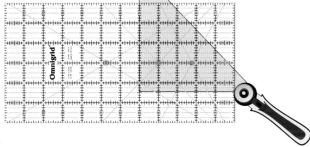

Cutting Diagrams

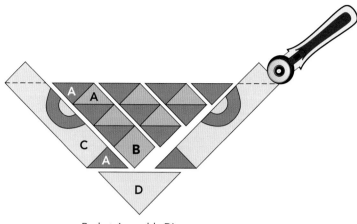

Basket Assembly Diagram

Block Assembly Diagram

Block Diagram

Block Assembly

1. Join 1 light gold print A triangle and 1 dark gold print A triangle to make a triangle-square. Make 5 triangle-squares.

2. Lay out triangle-squares, 4 dark gold print A triangles, and 1 light gold print B square as shown in *Basket Assembly Diagram.* Join into rows; join rows to complete basket.

3. Join 1 dark gold print A triangle to bottom of 1 tan print C rectangle. Appliqué handle on C rectangle. Join C rectangle to side of basket. Trim C rectangle as shown. Repeat for opposite side.

4. Add tan print D triangle to bottom of basket unit.

5. Referring to *Block Assembly Diagram,* appliqué leaves, stems, and flowers to E background triangle. Join background triangle to basket unit.

6. Add 1 medium blue #2 F triangle to each corner of block *(Block Diagram).*

Finishing

1. Layer backing, batting, and quilt top; baste. Quilt as desired. Quilt shown is outline quilted around flowers and basket, has vertical lines in the background, and a feather motif in each corner.

2. Frame block. (If you prefer, join 2¼"-wide strips into 1 continuous piece for straight-grain French-fold binding. Add binding to quilt.)

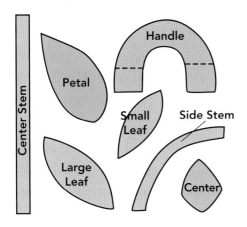

Center Stem

Petal

Handle

Small Leaf

Side Stem

Large Leaf

Center

> Patterns are reversed for use with fusible web.
> Add ³⁄₁₆" seam allowance for hand appliqué.

TRIED & TRUE

Judie made another version in a red-and-green color combination.

TIP: Center quilted block on cardboard back for picture frame. Using masking tape, secure block to frame back. Place desired mats over block. Put matted block in frame.

DESIGNER

Self-proclaimed computer junkie Judie Rothermel believes if she weren't involved in the quilting world, she would own a computer store. Judie has designed the Aunt Grace (named after Judie's aunt) fabric lines for Marcus Brothers. Over 1,000 different designs have been printed, and they are now becoming collector's items. ✳

QUILT BY **Jo Morton**.

Prairie Cabin Mini

Nebraskan Jo Morton has made dozens of Log Cabin quilts, playing with different sets, numbers of blocks, and border treatments. Miniatures are favorites with Jo because she can hand quilt them in no time at all.

PROJECT RATING: EASY
Size: 13½" × 18¼"
Blocks: 6 (4¾") Log Cabin blocks

MATERIALS

6" square red solid for block centers
6 (1" × 40") strips assorted light
prints for blocks
6 (1" × 40") strips assorted dark
prints for blocks
2 (1½" × 40") strips each of red
print and brown print for border
¼ yard red-and-black check for
binding
18" × 22" piece of backing fabric
18" × 22" piece of quilt batting

Cutting

Measurements include ¼" seam
allowances.
From red solid, cut:
• 6 (1¼") center squares.
From each light print strip, cut:
• 1 (1" × 1¼") #1 piece.
• 1 (1" × 1¾") #2 piece.
• 1 (1" × 2¼") #5 piece.
• 1 (1" × 2¾") #6 piece.
• 1 (1" × 3¼") #9 piece.
• 1 (1" × 3¾") #10 piece.
• 1 (1" × 4¼") #13 piece.
• 1 (1" × 4¾") #14 piece.
From each dark print strip, cut:
• 1 (1" × 1¾") #3 piece.
• 1 (1" × 2¼") #4 piece.
• 1 (1" × 2¾") #7 piece.
• 1 (1" × 3¼") #8 piece.
• 1 (1" × 3¾") #11 piece.
• 1 (1" × 4¼") #12 piece.

• 1 (1" × 4¾") #15 piece.
• 1 (1" × 5¼") #16 piece.
From red-and-black check, cut:
• 8 (2¼"-wide) bias strips. Join to
make about 80" of bias binding.

Block Assembly

1. Lay out pieces as shown in *Block Diagram*.
2. Join strips in numerical order
to complete 1 Log Cabin block.
Make 6 blocks.

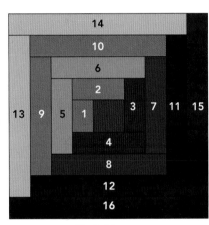

Block Diagram

Quilt Assembly

1. Lay out blocks as shown in *Quilt Top Assembly Diagram*.
2. Join blocks into rows; join rows
to complete quilt center.
3. Join 1 red print and 1 brown
print strip to make a strip set *(Strip Set Diagram)*. Make 2 strip sets.

Strip Set Diagram

4. From strip sets, cut 2 (14¾"-long)
side borders and 2 (14"-long) top
and bottom borders.
5. Add side borders to quilt. Add
top and bottom borders.

Finishing

1. Layer backing, batting, and quilt
top; baste. Quilt as desired. Quilt
shown was hand quilted with
concentric squares in the blocks
and a diagonal grid in the border.
2. Add binding to quilt.

Quilt Top Assembly Diagram

DESIGNER

Jo Morton began making quilts in 1980 and hasn't put down
her needle since. A quilt artist, author, teacher, and lecturer, Jo
designs fabrics for Andover Fabrics. She loves to make quilts in
the spirit of the nineteenth century. Jo lives in Nebraska City,
Nebraska, with her husband, Russ, and three cats. ✳

Go Fish

Surprise the fisherman in your life with this wall quilt to hang in his office or den.
Foundation piecing makes this quilt a snap to sew for a last minute Father's Day gift.

PROJECT RATING: INTERMEDIATE
Size: 16½" × 17"
Blocks: 8 (5¾" × 3") Fish blocks

MATERIALS

8 (3" × 8") rectangles of assorted
    rust, olive, gold, brown, and tan
    print or plaid fabrics for fish
8 (1½" × 40") strips of assorted rust,
    green, blue, gold, and tan solid
    fabrics for block backgrounds
⅜ yard dark blue print for inner
    border, outer border, and binding
⅛ yard olive green print for middle
    border and outer border squares
1 fat quarter★ for backing
18" × 20" piece of quilt batting
Black pearl cotton or embroidery
    thread for eyes, line, and hooks
Paper for foundations
★fat quarter = 18" × 20"

Cutting

Measurements include ¼" seam
allowances. Border strips are exact
length needed. You may want to
make them longer to allow for piecing
variations. Foundation patterns are on
page 51. For instructions and a video
on foundation piecing go to
www.FonsandPorter.com/pfp.

From dark blue, cut:
• 2 (1"-wide) strips. Cut strips to
    make 2 (1" × 13½") side inner
    borders and 2 (1" × 12") top and
    bottom inner borders.
• 2 (1½"-wide) strips. Cut strips to
    make 2 (1½" × 13½") side outer
    borders and 2 (1½" × 13") top and
    bottom outer borders, and 4 (1½")
    squares.
• 2 (2¼"-wide) strips for binding.

From olive green print, cut:
• 2 (1½"-wide) strips. Cut strips to
    make 2 (1½" × 17½") side middle
    borders, 2 (1½" × 13") top and
    bottom middle borders, and 4
    (1½") squares.

Block Assembly

1. Trace or photocopy 4 each of
fish unit A, B, and C foundation
patterns on page 51. Be sure to
include numbers on your tracings.
Make 4 reverse tracings of each
unit for fish that swim the opposite
direction.

2. Foundation piece units in
numerical order using print or
plaid fish fabrics for all areas
marked F and solid background
fabrics for all other areas.

3. Referring to *Block Assembly
Diagram*, join units A, B, and C,
pressing seam allowances toward
the tail of the fish. Make 4 Fish
blocks *(Block Diagram)* and 4
reverse Fish blocks.

Quilt Assembly

1. Referring to *Quilt Top Assembly
Diagram*, lay out Fish blocks as
shown. Join blocks into rows; join
rows to complete quilt center.

2. Add dark blue print inner borders
to top and bottom of quilt. Add
dark blue print inner borders to
sides of quilt.

3. Add olive print middle borders
to top and bottom of quilt. Add
dark blue outer borders to top and
bottom of quilt.

4. Add olive print side middle
borders.

5. Join 1 olive print 1½" square and
1 dark blue print 1½" square to
each end of dark blue print side
outer borders. Join to quilt.

Unit C   Unit B   Unit A

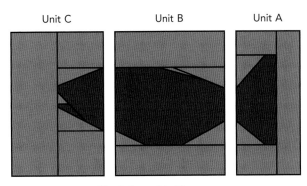

Block Assembly Diagram

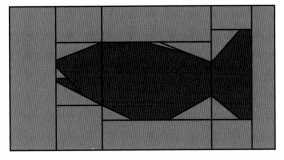

Block Diagram

Finishing

1. Refer to Unit C pattern for placement of embellishments on fish. Using pearl cotton or embroidery thread, make a French knot for eye of each fish. For fishing line, chain stitch or stem stitch along dotted line, adding 2 curved shapes at end of line for hook (photo on page 49).

2. Layer backing, batting, and quilt top; baste. Quilt as desired. Quilt shown was quilted in the ditch between fish and between borders.

3. Join 2¼"-wide dark blue print strips into 1 continuous piece for straight-grain French-fold binding. Add binding to quilt.

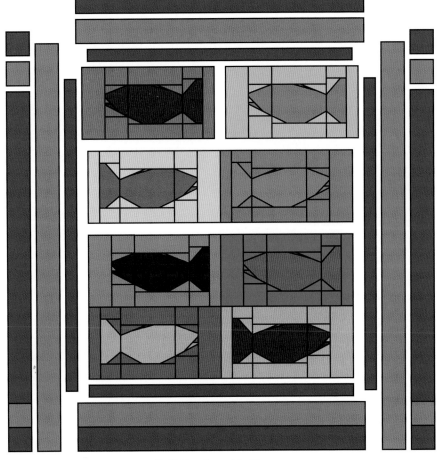

Quilt Top Assembly Diagram

DESIGNER

Mary Herschleb was first attracted to miniatures when she was a child making quilts for her dollhouse. As an adult, she began designing paper foundation quilt patterns and has turned her hobby into a business. ❋

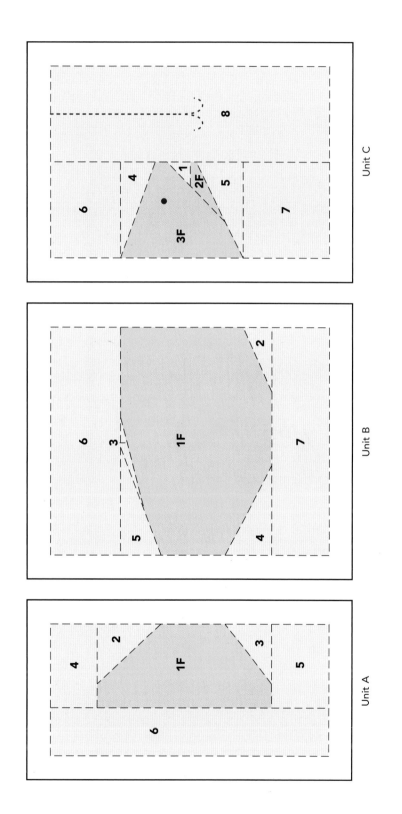

Unit C

Unit B

Unit A

EMBROIDERY BY **Leora Raikin**. BEADING BY **Betty Blais**.

Kuku Bird

Embroider this fun and fanciful bird inspired by the work of women of the Ndebele tribe in South Africa. Finish it as an embellished wallhanging, a pillow, or a framed work of art.

PROJECT RATING: EASY
Size: 12½" × 12½"
Blocks: 1 (7") Bird block

MATERIALS

1 pre-printed Bird block or
   10" square black solid for
   background.
Hand-dyed embroidery thread
1 fat eighth★ light brown print for
   inner border
1 fat eighth★ multi-color stripe for
   outer border
1 fat quarter★★ dark brown print for
   binding and border corners
1 fat quarter★★ backing fabric
Assortment of beads and sequins for
   embellishment
Beading thread
16" × 16" quilt batting
★fat eighth = 9" × 20"
★★fat quarter = 18" × 20"

Cutting

Pattern for embroidery is on page
53. Stitch diagrams are on page 54.
Measurements include ¼" seam
allowances.
From light brown print, cut:
• 2 (1"-wide) strips. From strips, cut
  2 (1" × 7½") side inner borders
  and 2 (1" × 8½") top and bottom
  inner borders.

From multi-color stripe, cut:

- 2 (2½"-wide) strips. From strips, cut 4 (2½" × 8½") outer borders.

From dark brown print, cut:

- 1 (2½"-wide) strip. From strip, cut 4 (2½") squares for outer border.
- 4 (2¼"-wide) strips for binding.

Block Assembly

1. Transfer embroidery design to background fabric.
2. Referring to photo, embroider bird block, using chain stitch and satin stitch as shown in diagrams on page 54. Trim block to 7½" square.

Quilt Assembly

1. Add side inner borders to block. Add top and bottom inner borders to block.
2. Add side outer borders to quilt center. Join 1 (2½") dark brown print square to each end of top and bottom outer borders. Add borders to quilt.
3. Referring to *Sew Easy: Bead Embellishments* on page 54 and photo on page 52, embellish as desired with beads and sequins.

Finishing

1. Layer backing, batting, and quilt top; baste. Quilt as desired. Quilt shown was quilted in the ditch.
2. Join 2¼"-wide dark brown print strips into 1 continuous piece for straight-grain French-fold binding. Add binding to quilt. ✳

Bead Embellishments

Beads and sequins added to a quilt give it extra dimension and character.
Try one of these basic beading techniques on your next project.

A

B

C

If desired, mark your design or bead placement on fabric with an erasable marking pen or chalk pencil. For best results, place work in a frame or hoop for beading. Use a quilting "between" needle, size 10 or 11, and Nymo size D beading thread or quilting thread.

Attaching Bugle Beads

1. Bring thread to top of work at point where 1 end of bead will be positioned.
2. Slide 1 bugle bead onto thread. Poke needle into fabric where opposite end of bead will be (*Photo A*), bringing needle underneath and back up at position where next bead will go. Repeat to attach remaining bugle beads. If desired, add seed beads at each end of bugle bead.

Attaching Seed Beads and Sequins

1. Bring thread to top of work at center of sequin position.
2. Slide 1 sequin and 1 seed bead onto thread. Poke needle through sequin and then into background (*Photo B*), bringing needle underneath and back up at position where next sequin and bead will go.

Attaching Round Beads

1. Bring thread to top of work at point where center of bead will be positioned.
2. Slide 1 round bead onto thread. Poke needle through fabric next to outside edge of bead (*Photo C*), bringing needle underneath and back up through center of bead. Poke needle through fabric next to outside edge of opposite side of bead. Repeat to add remaining round beads.

Satin Stitch

Chain Stitch

Stitch Diagrams

Springy Flowers

Designer Wendy Butler Berns created this lively wallhanging using simple, familiar shapes so other quilters would say, "I can do that." The shapes are fused to the background and embellished with textured threads and yarns.

PROJECT RATING: INTERMEDIATE
Size: 17½" × 21"

MATERIALS

1 fat quarter★★ light blue print for background

1 fat eighth★ bright turquoise print for inner border

1 fat quarter★★ bright pink print for outer border

2 (4" × 6") rectangles of green print fabric for leaves

8" squares of assorted bright green, yellow, orange, red, and pink prints for appliqué

Assorted cotton, rayon, and metallic threads in colors to match and contrast with appliqué

5 (12"-long) pieces of assorted green yarns for couched stems

Paper-backed fusible web

Tear-away stabilizer

Template material

⅝ yard backing fabric

2½-yard lengths of several yarns for yarn binding

22" × 25" piece quilt batting

★fat eighth = 9" × 20"

★★fat quarter = 18" × 20"

Cutting

Patterns for appliqué pieces and leaf template are on page 57. Follow manufacturer's instructions for using fusible web. Measurements include ¼" seam allowances. Border strips are exact length needed. You may want to make them longer to allow for piecing variations.

Quilt Top Assembly Diagram

From light blue print, cut:
• 1 (12" × 14½") rectangle for background.

From bright turquoise print, cut:
• 4 (1½"-wide) strips. From strips, cut 2 (1½" × 13½") side inner borders and 2 (1½" × 12") top and bottom inner borders.

From bright pink print, cut:
• 4 (3½"-wide) strips. From strips, cut 2 (3½" × 18") top and bottom outer borders and 2 (3½" × 15½") side outer borders.

From assorted bright prints, cut:
• Appliqué pieces as shown on page 57. (Do not cut leaves yet.)

Appliqué and Machine Embellishment

1. Fuse 2 (4" × 6") pieces of green fabric together, wrong sides facing.

Using leaf template, cut 5 leaves from fused fabric.

2. Referring to *Quilt Top Assembly Diagram* and photograph on page 55, arrange all appliqué pieces except fused leaves on background. Position long leaves even with the bottom edge of background rectangle. Remaining appliqué pieces should be at least 1½" from the outer edge of background. Fuse shapes in place.

3. Using tear-away stabilizer beneath background, attach fused leaves to background with stitched veins. Couch green yarn on background to make stems. See *Machine Embellishing and Quilting Ideas* on page 59 for stitching ideas.

4. Remove excess stabilizer. Trim background to 10" × 13½".

Quilt Assembly

1. Add turquoise print inner borders to sides of quilt. Add top and bottom inner borders to quilt.

2. Repeat for pink print outer borders.

Finishing

1. Layer backing, batting, and quilt top; baste. Quilt as desired. Quilt shown was quilted in the ditch around borders and with random swirls in background and angles and squares in outer border.

2. Add binding to quilt. Refer to *Sew Easy: Yarn Binding* on page 58 for instructions to make and attach yarn binding.

DESIGNER

Wendy Butler Berns of Lake Mills, Wisconsin, has taught and lectured about the art of quilting since 1997. Her quilts—fluctuating between traditional with a twist and contemporary art quilts—appear regularly in juried shows, galleries, and private collections across the United States. ✳

Cut 1

Cut 1

Cut 1

Cut 1
from template
material

Cut 1

Cut 3

Cut 2

Cut 3

Cut 1

Cut 4

Cut 2

Cut 1

Cut 1

Cut 1

Patterns are shown full size and are reversed for use with fusible web.

 **Sew Easy**™

Yarn Binding

Instead of traditional binding on a small wallhanging, try Wendy Butler Berns' quick and simple couched yarn binding. Use a single strand of thick yarn or twist several thinner yarns together to create a stunning effect.

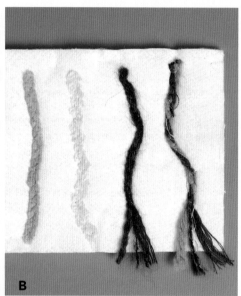

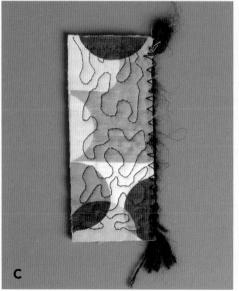

1. Trim quilt edges so all layers are even (*Photo A*).
2. If using several yarns, twist strands together (*Photo B*).
3. Put a darning foot on your sewing machine and set stitch to a wide zigzag.
4. Hold the twisted yarns next to the quilt edge and use either monofilament or decorative thread to catch both the yarn and the quilt edge with a wide zigzag stitch (*Photo C*).
5. Stitch around edge twice to be sure the quilt edges and yarns are securely fastened (*Photo D*).

Machine Embellishing and Quilting Ideas

Embellish the pink flower with green dots. Outline quilt around the flower shape and stitch continuous circles on the flower in pink thread.

Use blue metallic thread to make spirals on the butterfly wings. Outline quilt around the butterfly and stitch antennae in purple thread.

Embroider purple flower centers on the red flower. Quilt the petals with an allover clamshell design.

Stitch freehand swirling centers on the red flower. Outline quilt around the flower and quilt it with freehand leaves.

Stitch veins on dimensional leaves to attach them to the quilt top. Thin stems are made from yarn couched to the background. Appliqué stems are quilted with continuous loops.

The yellow-and-pink flower has multiple lines of stitching in a spiral design on each color.

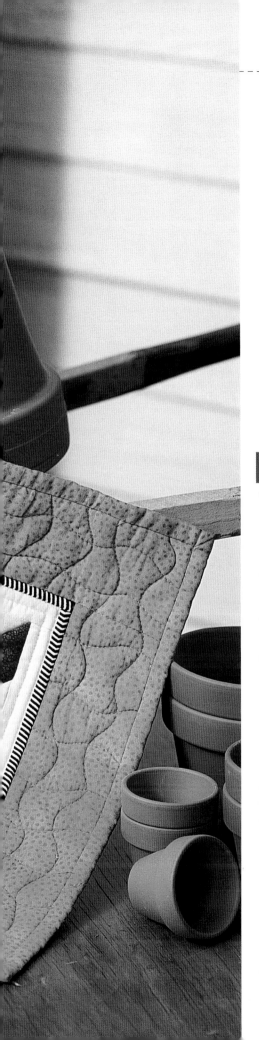

Tulip Mini

The bright tulips in this springy wallhanging seem to pop off the fabric. Foundation piecing makes this project go together quickly.

PROJECT RATING: INTERMEDIATE

Size: 17½" × 11½"

Blocks: 5 (2" × 6") Tulip blocks

MATERIALS

1 fat quarter★★ white print for block background and sashing

⅜ yard turquoise print for outer border and binding

1 fat eighth★ black-and-white stripe for inner border

10 (6") squares assorted bright prints in pink, yellow, orange, green, red, purple, and blue for tulips

2 (6") squares green prints for stems and leaves

10 (3") squares multi-colored prints for flowerpots and flowerpot rims

Paper for foundations

1 fat quarter★★ backing fabric

20" × 14" piece quilt batting

★fat eighth = 9" × 20"

★★fat quarter = 18" × 20"

Cutting

Foundation patterns are on page 63. Measurements include ¼" seam allowances. Border strips are exact length needed. You may want to make them longer to allow for piecing variations.

From white print, cut:

• 4 (1"-wide) strips. From strips, cut 2 (1" × 13½") horizontal sashing strips and 6 (1" × 6½") vertical sashing strips.

• Use remaining fabric for foundation piecing.

From turquoise print, cut:

• 2 (2½"-wide) strips. From strips, cut 2 (2½" × 18") top and bottom outer borders and 2 (2½" × 8") side outer borders.

• 2 (2¼"-wide) strips for binding.

From black-and-white stripe, cut:

• 3 (¾"-wide) strips. From strips, cut 2 (¾" × 14") top and bottom inner borders and 2 (¾" × 7½") side inner borders.

Block Assembly

1. Trace or photocopy 3 sets of foundation patterns for Section A, Section B, and Section C on page 63. Using assorted bright print fabrics for flowers, green prints for leaves and stems, multi-colored

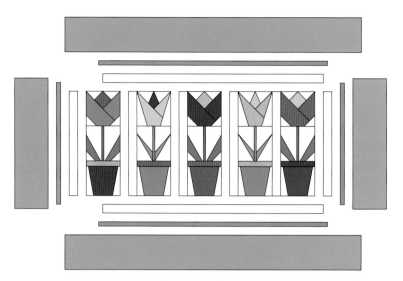

Quilt Top Assembly Diagram

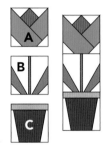

Block 1 Diagrams

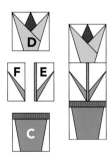

Block 2 Diagrams

prints for flowerpots, and white print for background, foundation piece each section in numerical order.

2. Join Sections A, B, and C to complete Block 1 *(Block 1 Diagrams)*. Make 3 Block 1.

3. Trace or photocopy 2 sets of foundation patterns for Section C, Section D, Section E, and Section F on page 63. Foundation piece each section in numerical order.

4. Join Sections as shown in Block 2 Diagrams. Make 2 Block 2.

Quilt Assembly

1. Referring to *Quilt Top Assembly Diagram*, lay out blocks and sashing strips as shown; join to complete quilt center.

2. Add black-and-white stripe side inner borders to quilt center. Add black-and-white stripe top and bottom inner borders to quilt. Repeat for turquoise print outer borders.

Finishing

1. Layer backing, batting, and quilt top; baste. Quilt as desired. Quilt shown was quilted in the ditch around the tulips, with straight lines through the centers of the sashing strips, and with a wavy grid in the outer borders.

2. Join 2¼"-wide turquoise print strips into 1 continuous piece for straight-grain French-fold binding. Add binding to quilt.

DESIGNER

Leisa Breheny of Greenfield, Iowa, began quilting in 1989. She enjoys designing patterns for small projects that she can make for gifts.

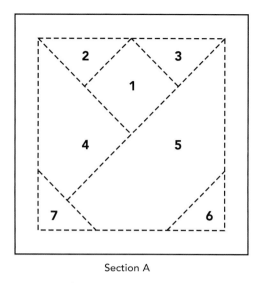

Section A

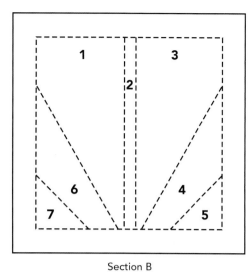

Section B

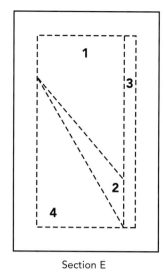

Section E

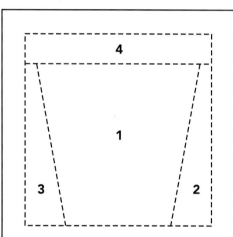

Section C

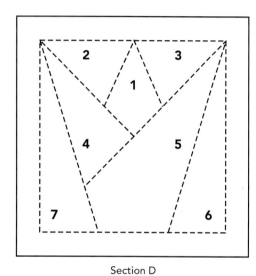

Section D

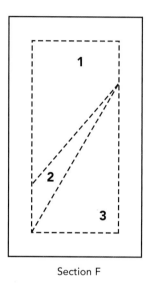

Section F

TRIED & TRUE

We used a variety of pink prints and just one green for our version. The fabrics shown here are from several collections by Northcott. ✳

This Flower
IS FOR YOU

Caroline Kearney says, "I am fascinated with black-and-white fabrics used with bright colors in quilts." She combined that fascination with her love for cats to create this little quilt.

PROJECT RATING: INTERMEDIATE
Size: 25" × 22"

MATERIALS

1 fat quarter★ white solid for block background and cat face

1 fat eighth★★ black solid for cat head, legs, and tail

6" square gray print for vase

1 fat eighth★★ green print for leaves and stems

4" square each of pink, red, and fuchsia prints for flowers

4" square yellow print for flower centers

1 fat quarter★ black-and-white print for cat body and border corners

⅜ yard black-and-white check for borders

Paper-backed fusible web

Permanent markers for cat face

¾ yard backing fabric

¼ yard black-and-white stripe for binding

29" × 26" piece of quilt batting

★ fat quarter = 18" × 20"

★★ fat eighth = 9" × 20"

Cutting

Measurements include ¼" seam allowances. Appliqué patterns are on pages 66–67. Follow manufacturer's instructions for using fusible web.

From white solid, cut:

• 1 (17½" × 14½") rectangle for block background.

• 1 Cat Face.

From black solid, cut:

• 1 Cat Head.

• 2 (⅝" × 4") rectangles for Cat Legs.

• 1 Cat Tail.

From gray print, cut:

• 1 Vase.

From green print, cut:

• 1 Left Stem.

• 1 Middle Stem.

• 1 Right Stem.

• 1 Stem to tuck under cat's mouth.

• 14 Leaves.

From each pink, red, and fuchsia print, cut:

• 1 Flower.

From yellow print, cut:

• 3 Flower Centers.

From black-and-white print, cut:

• 1 Cat Body.

• 4 (4½") squares for border corners.

From black-and-white check, cut:

• 2 (4½"-wide) strips. From strips, cut 2 (4½" × 17½") top and bottom borders and 2 (4½" × 14½") side borders.

From black-and-white stripe, cut:

• 3 (2¼"-wide) strips for binding.

Quilt Assembly

Refer to photograph on page 65 when positioning appliqué pieces.

1. Add side border strips to background rectangle.

2. Add 1 (4½") black-and-white print square to each end of top and bottom borders. Add borders to top and bottom of quilt.

3. Position Cat Head, Legs, Tail, and Body on background, tucking Head, Legs, and Tail under Body piece. Fuse in place.

4. Referring to pattern on page 67, draw cat face with permanent markers.

5. Position Cat Face on head. Tuck stem under mouth. Fuse in place.

6. Position Vase, Stems, and Leaves on background, tucking Stems and bottom leaves on middle stem under top of vase. Fuse in place.

7. Position Flowers and Flower Centers on Stems. Fuse in place.

8. Blanket stitch around all appliqué pieces, using matching thread.

Finishing

1. Layer backing, batting, and quilt top; baste. Quilt as desired. Quilt shown was outline quilted around the appliqué shapes and stippled in the background. The borders are quilted with curves and loops.

2. Join 2¼"-wide black-and-white stripe strips into 1 continuous piece for straight-grain French-fold binding. Add binding to quilt.

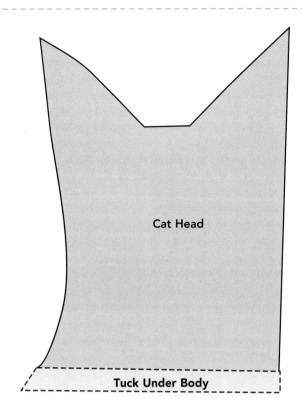

Cat Head

Tuck Under Body

Patterns are shown full size and are reversed for use with fusible web.

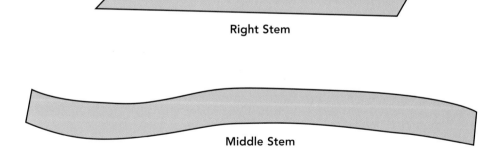

Right Stem

Middle Stem

DESIGNER

Born and educated in Germany, Caroline Kearney emigrated to the USA in 1962. In 1990 she began quilting and knew immediately that she was going to make quilts for the rest of her life. She enjoys making one-of-a-kind art quilts and creates quilt designs for others to make from her line of commercial patterns. ✳

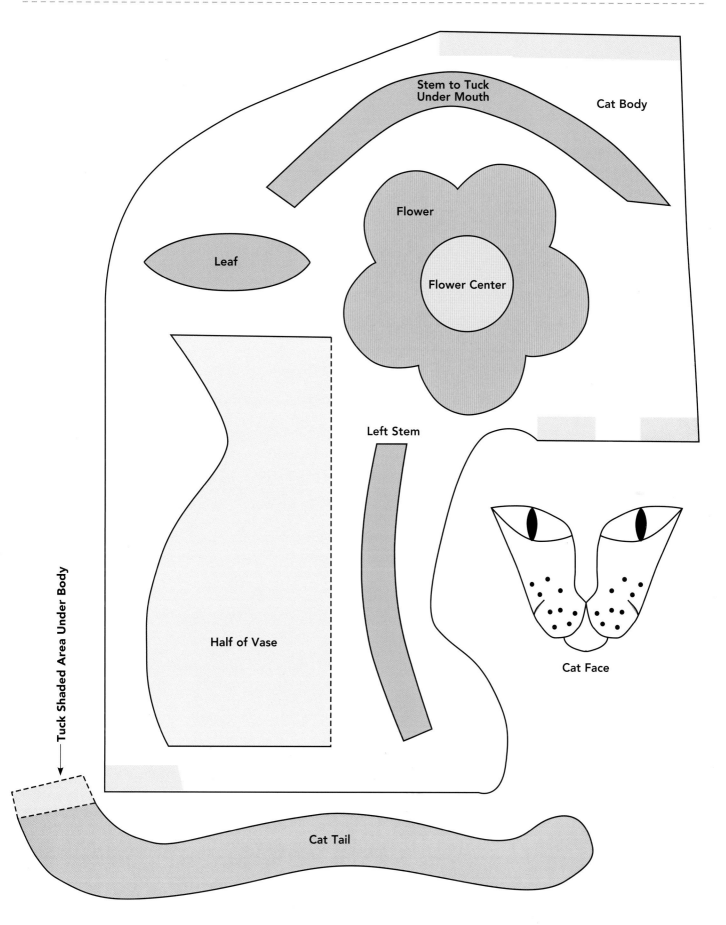

Stem to Tuck
Under Mouth

Cat Body

Flower

Flower Center

Leaf

Left Stem

Half of Vase

Cat Face

Tuck Shaded Area Under Body

Cat Tail

GINGER'S
Flower Garden

Designers Keri Duke and Ginger White combined five easy blocks in this pieced garden wallhanging. Ginger used a variety of embroidery designs for the quilting.

PROJECT RATING: INTERMEDIATE
Size: 35" × 29¼"

MATERIALS

NOTE: Fabrics in the quilt shown are from the Fairy Frost collection by Mark Hordyszynski for Michael Miller Fabrics.

5 fat eighths★ assorted bright prints for blocks

5 fat eighths★ assorted pastel prints for blocks

1¼ yards cream print for background

¾ yard green print for blocks and setting triangles

1 yard backing fabric

Craft-size quilt batting

★ fat eighth = 9" × 20"

Cutting

Measurements include ¼" seam allowances.

From each bright fat eighth, cut:

• 1 (2⅞"-wide) strip. From strip, cut 2 (2⅞") squares. Cut squares in half diagonally to make 4 half-square A triangles.

• 1 (1½"-wide) strip. From strip, cut 12 (1½") B squares.

From each pastel fat eighth, cut:

• 1 (2⅞"-wide) strip. From strip, cut 2 (2⅞") squares and 2 (2½") C squares. Cut 2⅞" squares in half diagonally to make 4 half-square A triangles.

• 1 (1½"-wide) strip. From strip, cut 12 (1½") B squares.

From cream print, cut:

• 1 (8"-wide) strip. From strip, cut 3 (8") squares and 1 (7⅝") square. Cut 7⅝" square in half diagonally to make 2 corner setting triangles. Cut 8" squares in half diagonally in both directions to make 12 quarter-square setting triangles (2 are extra).

• 3 (4½"-wide) strips. From strips, cut 22 (4½") F squares. Cut 5 squares in half diagonally to make 10 half-square D triangles.

• 1 (2½"-wide) strip. From strip, cut 14 (2½") C squares.

• 3 (2¼"-wide) strips for binding.

• 2 (1½"-wide) strips for strip set.

From green print, cut:

• 1 (8"-wide) strip. From strip, cut 1 (8") square and 1 (7⅝") square.

Cut 7⅝" square in half diagonally to make 2 corner setting triangles. Cut 8" square in half diagonally in both directions to make 4 quarter-square setting triangles.

• 1 (2½"-wide) strip. From strip, cut 10 (2½") C squares.

• 2 (2¼"-wide) strips for binding.

• 2 (1½"-wide) strips for strip set.

• 1 (1"-wide) strip. From strip, cut 5 (1" × 6½") E rectangles.

Block Assembly

1. Choose 1 set of 4 matching pastel print B squares, 2 C squares, and 4 A triangles. Choose 1 set of 4 matching bright print B squares and 4 A triangles.

2. Join 2 bright B squares and 2 pastel B squares to make 1 Four Patch Unit (*Four Patch Unit Diagrams*). Make 2 Four Patch Units.

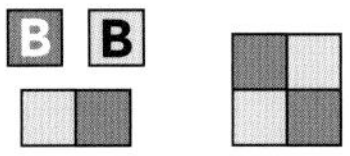

Four Patch Unit Diagrams

Quilt Top Assembly Diagram

3. Join 2 Four Patch Units and 2 C squares to make 1 Double Four Patch block *(Double Four Patch Block Diagrams)*. Make 5 Double Four Patch blocks, 1 in each color.

Double Four Patch Block Diagrams

4. Join 1 bright A triangle and 1 pastel A triangle to make a triangle-square *(Triangle-Square Diagrams)*. Make 4 matching triangle-squares.

Triangle-Square Diagrams

5. Join triangle-squares to make 1 Pinwheel block *(Pinwheel Block Diagram)*. Make 5 Pinwheel blocks, 1 in each color.

Pinwheel Block Diagram

6. Lay out 16 assorted pastel and bright B squares. Join into rows; join rows to make 1 Sixteen Patch Block 1 *(Sixteen Patch Block 1 Diagrams)*. Make 5 Sixteen Patch Block 1.

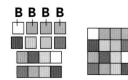

Sixteen Patch Block 1 Diagrams

7. Join 2 green print C squares and 2 cream print C squares to make

1 Four Patch Block 1. *(Four Patch Block 1 Diagrams)*. Make 4 Four Patch Block 1.

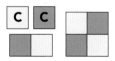

Four Patch Block 1 Diagrams

8. In a similar manner, make 2 Four Patch Block 2, using 1 green print C square and 3 cream print C squares. *(Four Patch Block 2 Diagrams)*.

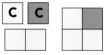

Four Patch Block 2 Diagrams

9. Join 2 cream D triangles and 1 green E rectangle, matching centers. Trim ends of E rectangle even with sides of triangles to make 1 Stem Unit *(Stem Unit Diagrams)*. Make 5 Stem Units.

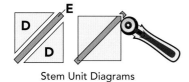

Stem Unit Diagrams

10. Join 2 (1½"-wide) green print strips and 2 (1½"-wide) cream strips as shown in *Strip Set Diagram*. From strip set, cut 24 (1½"-wide) segments.

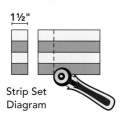

Strip Set Diagram

Sew **Smart**™

When joining strips for strip sets, alternate sewing direction from strip to strip. This keeps strip sets straight. —Liz

---

11. Join 4 strip set segments to make 1 Sixteen Patch Block 2 *(Sixteen Patch Block 2 Diagrams)*. Make 6 Sixteen Patch Block 2.

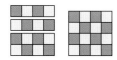

Sixteen Patch Block 2 Diagrams

Quilt Assembly

1. Referring to *Quilt Top Assembly Diagram*, lay out blocks, Stem Units, cream F squares, and side setting triangles as shown. Join into diagonal rows; join rows. **NOTE:** Setting triangles are oversized.

2. Add green print and cream print corner triangles to quilt.

Finishing

1. Layer backing, batting, and quilt top; baste. Quilt as desired. Quilt shown was quilted with leaves in the bottom portion, and with assorted flower designs in the upper portion. *(Quilting Diagram)*.

2. Join 2¼"-wide cream print strips into 1 continuous piece for straight-grain French-fold binding. Repeat for green binding strips.

3. Referring to quilt photo on page 69, add cream binding to top and sides of quilt. Trim ends at desired location, leaving a ¼" seam allowance. Join green print binding strip to 1 end of cream binding on right side of quilt. Continue sewing binding to quilt. Trim end of green binding, leaving a ¼" seam allowance. Join ends; finish stitching binding to quilt.

Quilting Diagram

DESIGNER

Retired school teacher Ginger White wanted to make a wallhanging that she could quilt with her embroidery machine. She and her friend Keri Duke created this design using simple blocks and sparkly, bright fabrics. ✳

Primitive Checkerboard

Antique checkerboards with their wonderful painted designs were the inspiration for this folk art quilt made with flannel and homespun fabrics.

PROJECT RATING: INTERMEDIATE

Size: 38½" × 38½"

MATERIALS

1½ yards black plaid

¼ yard tan print

¼ yard orange plaid

½ yard red stripe

½ yard gold print

¼ yard dark green plaid

8 fat eighths★ assorted light green, black, tan, orange, and red plaids, stripes, and prints for appliqué pieces, Stars, and Flying Geese Units

Paper-backed fusible web

1¼ yards backing fabric

Crib-size quilt batting

★fat eighth = 9" × 20"

Cutting

Measurements include ¼" seam allowances. Border strips are exact length needed. You may want to make them longer to allow for piecing variations. Patterns for appliqué are on page 76. Follow manufacturer's instructions for using fusible web.

From black plaid, cut:

- 1 (6⅜"-wide) strip. From strip, cut 2 (6⅜") squares. Cut squares in half diagonally to make 4 half-square C triangles.
- 4 (6"-wide) strips. From strips, cut 4 (6" × 28") outer borders.
- 7 (2½"-wide) strips for strip sets and binding.
- 2 (1¼"-wide) strips. From strips, cut 2 (1¼" × 16½") side inner borders and 2 (1¼" × 18") top and bottom inner borders.

From tan print, cut:

- 2 (2½"-wide) strips for strip sets.

From orange plaid, cut:

- 1 (5½"-wide) strip. From strip, cut 1 (5½" × 23") rectangle for appliqué border background.

From red stripe, cut:

- 1 (6⅜"-wide) strip. From strip, cut 2 (6⅜") squares. Cut squares in half diagonally to make 4 half-square C triangles.
- 1 (5½"-wide) strip. From strip, cut 1 (5½" × 10½") rectangle for Flying Geese border.
- 1 (3"-wide) strip. From strip, cut 10 (3") B squares.

2½"

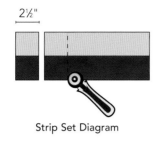

Strip Set Diagram

Flying Geese Unit Diagrams

Checkerboard Assembly Diagram

Flower Border
Assembly Diagram

Star Border Assembly Diagram

Border Corner Diagram

From gold print, cut:

- 1 (5½"-wide) strip. From strip, cut 1 (5½" × 10½") rectangle for Flying Geese border.
- 2 (3"-wide) strips. From strips, cut 14 (3") B squares.

From dark green plaid, cut:

- 1 (5½"-wide) strip. From strip, cut 1 (5½" × 18") rectangle for star border background.

From light green fat eighth, cut:

- 1 (1½" × 20") strip for stem. Fold strip in thirds, press, and hand baste fold in place to prepare stem for appliqué.

From remaining assorted fat eighths, cut a total of:

- 3 Stars.
- 12 (3" × 5½") A rectangles.
- 6 Leaves.
- 1 Flower.
- 1 Flower Center.

Center Assembly

1. Join 1 black plaid strip and 1 tan print strip as shown in *Strip Set Diagram*. Make 2 strip sets. From strip sets, cut 32 (2½") segments.
2. Join segments as shown in *Checkerboard Assembly Diagram* to complete quilt center.

Flying Geese Borders Assembly

1. Referring to *Flying Geese Unit Diagrams*, place 1 gold print B square atop 1 print A rectangle, right sides facing. Stitch diagonally from corner to corner as shown. Trim ¼" beyond stitching. Press open to reveal triangle. Repeat for opposite corner to complete 1 Flying Geese Unit. Make 7 Flying Geese Units using gold print B squares and assorted print A rectangles, and 5 Flying Geese Units using red stripe B squares and assorted print A rectangles.
2. Lay out 7 gold Flying Geese Units and gold print border rectangle as shown in *Quilt Top Assembly Diagram* on page 75. Join pieces to complete side Flying Geese Border.
3. In a similar manner, make top Flying Geese border using 5 red Flying Geese Units and red stripe border rectangle.

Appliqué Border Assembly

1. Referring to *Flower Border Assembly Diagram*, position vine and appliqué pieces on orange plaid border rectangle. Fuse pieces in place.
2. Machine stitch around appliqué pieces.

Star Border Assembly

1. Referring to *Star Border Assembly Diagram*, position 3 stars on green plaid border rectangle. Fuse stars in place.

2. Machine stitch around stars.

Quilt Assembly

1. Add black plaid side inner borders to quilt center as shown in *Quilt Top Assembly Diagram*. Add top and bottom inner borders to quilt.

2. Referring to *Quilt Top Assembly Diagram*, add Star border to bottom of quilt. Add Flower border to left side of quilt. Add red stripe Flying Geese border to top of quilt. Add gold print Flying Geese border to right side of quilt.

3. Add black plaid side outer borders to quilt.

4. Join 1 black plaid C triangle and 1 red stripe C triangle to make 1 border corner *(Border Corner Diagram)*. Make 4 border corners.

5. Add 1 Border Corner to each end of top and bottom black plaid outer borders. Add borders to quilt.

Finishing

1. Layer backing, batting, and quilt top; baste. Quilt as desired. Quilt shown was quilted in the ditch in the center and pieced borders, outline quilted around appliqué, and with freehand loops in the outer border *(Quilting Diagram)*.

2. Join 2½"-wide black plaid strips into 1 continuous piece for straight-grain French-fold binding. Add binding to quilt.

Quilt Top Assembly Diagram

Quilting Diagram

Patterns are shown full size and are reversed for use with fusible web. Add ³⁄₁₆" seam allowance for hand appliqué.

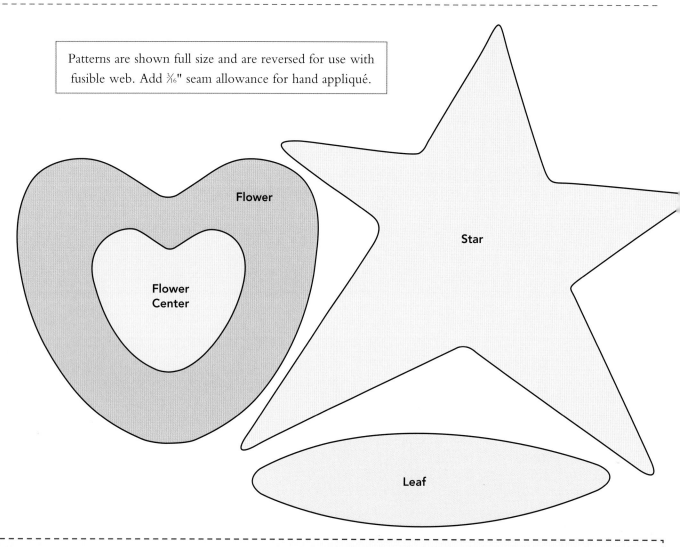

Flower

Flower Center

Star

Leaf

TRIED & TRUE

Grab some 1930s reproduction prints from your stash and make a bright and cheery version of this wallhanging.

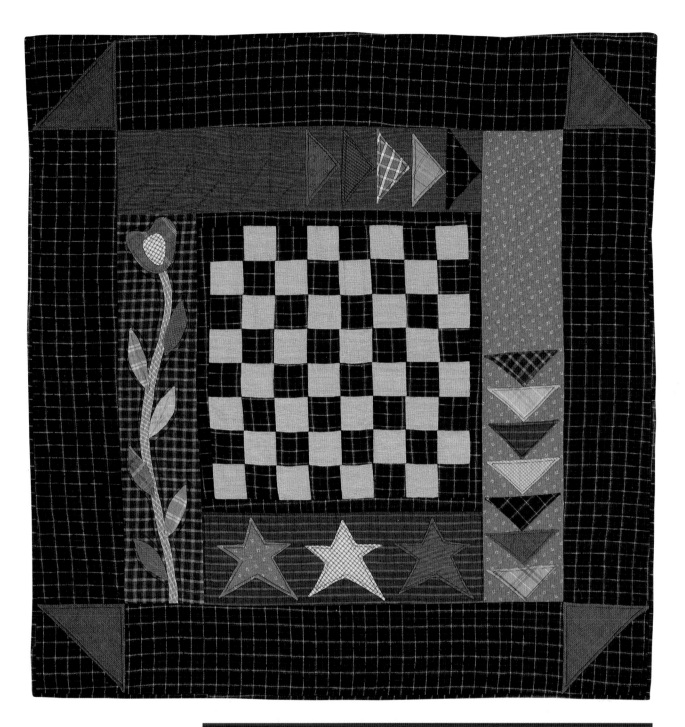

DESIGNER

Nancy Moore is especially fond of the primitive folk art look. She lives in the mountains of Montana, and can be reached through her blog www.tominerfolkart.blogspot.com. ✳

Quillow

A quillow is a quilted throw that folds up into a pillow.
The Fons & Porter staff has had a lot of fun making quillows as gifts for family and friends.

PROJECT RATING: EASY
Size: 39½" × 65"

MATERIALS

2 yards mottled tan print for quillow back

2 yards floral print for quillow front

2 pre-printed panels (16" square) for pocket **OR** 2 fat quarters★ coordinating print for pocket

Twin-size quilt batting **OR** 2 yards flannel or fleece for batting (If you use flannel or fleece, you will need a 16" square of batting for pocket.)

Sewing machine with walking foot
★fat quarter = 18" × 20"

Cutting

Measurements include ¼" seam allowances.

From mottled tan print, cut:
• 1 (40" × 65½") rectangle for quillow back.

From floral print, cut:
• 1 (44" × 70") rectangle for quillow front.

From each pre-printed panel (OR fat quarter), cut:
• 1 (16") square for pocket.

From batting (OR flannel or fleece), cut:
• 1 (46" × 72") rectangle.
• 1 (16") square.

Quillow Assembly

1. Place 2 pocket squares right sides together. Place paired squares atop batting square; pin. Stitch around three outer edges, leaving one side open to turn. If pocket has a directional design, leave opening at bottom edge of pocket.

2. Trim corners. Turn pocket right side out. Quilt, if desired.

3. Referring to *Quillow Assembly Diagrams*, with right sides facing, center pocket along bottom edge of quillow back piece, aligning raw edges. Machine baste in place. **NOTE:** The side of the pocket that is placed facing the quillow back will become the front of the pillow when the quillow is folded up.

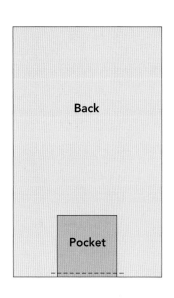
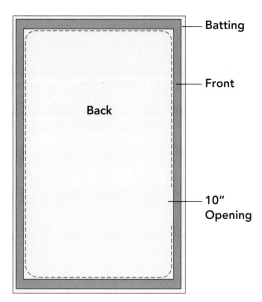

Quillow Assembly Diagrams

SIZE OPTIONS

Use this formula to make a quillow any size you like:

1. Determine the pillow size you want. **2.** Cut quillow back width 2" narrower than 3 times the size of the pillow. **3.** Cut quillow back length no more than 4 times the size of the pillow. **4.** Cut the front slightly larger than the back; cut the batting slightly larger than the front.

Example: For a 10" pillow, cut the back 28" wide (3 × 10" = 30"; 30" − 2" = 28") and 40" long (4 × 10" = 40").

Quilting Diagram

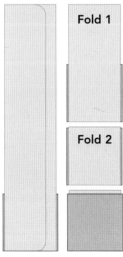

Fold 1

Fold 2

Folding Diagrams

4. Place quillow front atop batting rectangle, right side up; place quillow back atop quillow front, right sides facing. Use a cup or similar round object as a guide to mark rounded corners. Pin; stitch around outer edges, rounding corners. Leave a 10" opening on one side for turning.

Sew **Smart**™

Before stitching, put a 10"-long piece of masking tape along the edge of the quillow back where you plan to leave an opening. The tape will remind you not to stitch that section. —Marianne

5. Trim excess fabric. Turn quillow right side out through opening. Whipstitch opening closed.

6. Referring to *Quilting Diagram*, stitch through all layers, stitching

pocket down; continue stitching to opposite edge of quillow.

Sew **Smart**™

A great way to mark the stitching lines for the two lines of quilting that will hold the layers together is to fold and lightly press the quillow front fabric, pressing two lengthwise guidelines. —Liz

Folding Quillow

1. Referring to *Folding Diagrams*, turn the quillow over so the pocket is underneath. Fold lengthwise along quilting lines.

2. Fold the quillow twice as shown.

3. Turn the pocket right side out, tucking the folded quillow into the pocket to make a pillow.

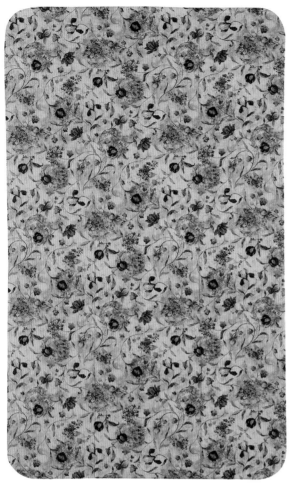

Quillow Front

Quillow Back

TRIED & TRUE

Fons & Porter staff members made a variety of quillows.

Left: Marianne Fons used a coordinating floral print and stripe in bright colors. **Center:** Liz Porter used a patchwork block for her pocket and chenille for the back of her quillow to make it even more snuggly. **Right:** Alison Ripperger chose 2 fabrics with construction equipment motifs. ❋

Yo-Yo Basket
PILLOW

Inspired by an antique pillow that belongs to a friend, Evalee Waltz made hers from reproduction fabrics. She used decorative buttons for the centers of some flowers.

PROJECT RATING: EASY

Size: 19" × 19" without ruffle

MATERIALS

⅝ yard cream solid for pillow front

1½ yards pink print for ruffle and pillow back

⅜ yard pink solid for basket yo-yos

1 fat eighth★ green solid for stems

14 (5") squares assorted pastel prints for yo-yos

Polyester fiberfill for stuffing pillow

2 (½"-diameter) yellow buttons for medium flower centers

★fat eighth = 9" × 20"

Cutting

Measurements include ¼" seam allowances. Patterns for yo-yo circles are on page 85.

From cream solid, cut:

• 1 (19½") square for pillow front.

From pink print, cut:

• 5 (6"-wide) strips for ruffle.

• 1 (19½") square for pillow back.

From pink solid, cut:

• 61 small circles for basket yo-yos.

From green solid, cut:

• 7 (1¼"-wide) bias strips for stems. Fold bias strips in thirds lengthwise, press, and hand baste fold in place to prepare stems for appliqué.

From pastel print squares, cut:

• 11 tiny circles for yo-yos (cut 6 from 1 fabric and 1 from yellow print for cluster flower).

• 3 small circles for yo-yos.

• 6 medium circles for yo-yos.

• 1 large circle for yo-yo.

Pillow Top Assembly

1. Referring to *Sew Easy: Making Yo-Yos* on page 84, make 61 pink solid yo-yos from small circles. Join yo-yos in 1 row of 3, 2 rows of 5, 1 row of 7, 1 row of 9, and 1 row of 11 yo-yos for basket. Join 21 yo-yos to make basket handle.

Sew **Smart**™

To join yo-yos, place 2 with right (gathered) sides facing. Using thread that blends with fabrics, whipstitch yo-yos together along one side. —Liz

2. To make basket, whipstitch rows of yo-yos together as shown in *Basket Diagram* on page 84. Center basket on pillow top, placing bottom of basket approximately 2" from bottom edge. Pin basket to pillow front. Pin handle strip in place. Wait to tack basket and handle to background until all flowers and stems are stitched in place.

3. Join 1 tiny yellow print yo-yo and 6 matching tiny yo-yos to make cluster flower, placing yellow yo-yo in center.

4. Referring to *Basket Diagram* on page 84, arrange bias stems, small, medium, and large yo-yos, and cluster flower on background square. Trim stems to desired lengths, concealing ends of stems under basket and flowers. Appliqué stems in place by hand or machine. Pin flower yo-yos in place.

5. Place a yo-yo or button atop each medium and large yo-yo flower for flower centers. Use remaining tiny yo-yos for centers of medium yo-yo flowers and remaining small yo-yo as center of large flower. Stitch center yo-yo or button

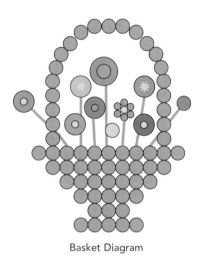

Basket Diagram

through all layers to hold pieces in place. Stitch center of cluster flower to background.

6. Stitch basket and handle yo-yos to background.

Pillow Finishing

1. Join 6"-wide pink print strips end to end to form loop for ruffle. Fold ruffle in half with wrong sides facing so it is 3" wide; press. Divide ruffle into 4 equal sections; mark divisions with pins. Run gathering thread around ruffle loop, a scant ¼" from raw edges.

2. Draw around a mug or large glass to mark rounded corners on right side of pillow top. Use pins to mark centers of pillow sides. Gather ruffle so that ¼ of ruffle is distributed along each quadrant of pillow top. Aligning raw edges of ruffle with edges of pillow top and rounded corner markings, pin ruffle in place. Baste ruffle to pillow top.

3. Place pillow top atop pillow back, right sides facing; pin. Working with wrong side of pillow top facing up so you can use basting stitching as stitching guide, stitch pillow top to pillow back, leaving an 8"-long opening along 1 side to turn pillow. Turn pillow right side out. Stuff pillow with fiberfill. Whipstitch opening closed.

Sew Easy™   Making Yo-Yos

Follow these simple steps to make yo-yos for *Yo-Yo Basket Pillow* on page 82.

1. Cut circle using pattern on page 85.
2. Turn under raw edge of circle ¼" to wrong side and take small running stitches around edge through both layers (*Photo A*). Use quilting thread or other strong thread that will not break when gathering.
3. Pull thread to gather circle with right side of fabric facing out. Make a knot to hold circle closed. Gathered side is front of yo-yo (*Photo B*).

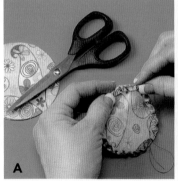

A

B

Sew Smart™
Do not make running stitches too small. Longer stitches make the circle easier to gather, and the "hole" smaller.
—Marianne

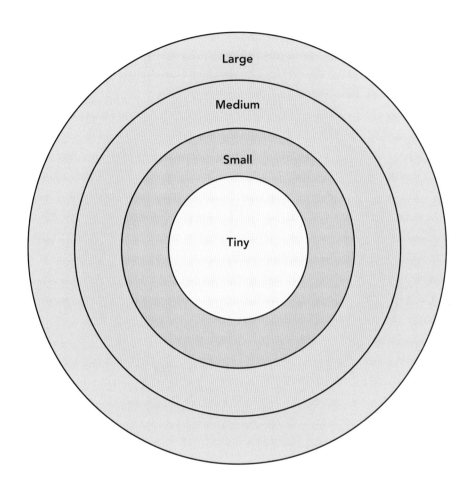

Large

Medium

Small

Tiny

DESIGNER

 Evalee Waltz learned to sew at the age of nine by watching her mother and grandmother. After meeting Marianne and Liz in 1978, Evalee became actively involved with the Heritage Quilters, and eventually became an employee of Fons & Porter. ✳

SIZE OPTION: YO-YO BASKET WALLHANGING

Make a yo-yo basket wallhanging with a folk art look. We chose fabrics from Bound to the Prairie 2 by Kansas Troubles for Moda.

PROJECT RATING: EASY
Size: 26¼" × 26¼"

MATERIALS

1 fat quarter★★ tan print
⅜ yard gold print
½ yard black print
⅜ yard black solid for basket yo-yos
Red print, gold print, and blue print scraps for yo-yos
1 fat eighth★ green print for stems
⅜ yard binding fabric
⅞ yard backing fabric
30" × 30" piece quilt batting
★fat eighth = 9" × 20"
★★fat quarter = 18" × 20"

Cutting

From tan print fat quarter, cut:

• 1 (13½") square.

From gold print, cut:

• 2 (10") squares. Cut squares in half diaonally to make 4 corner settting triangles.

From black print, cut:

• 3 (4½"-wide) strips. From strips, cut 2 (4½" × 26¾") top and bottom border strips and 2 (4½" × 18¾") side border stips.

From black solid, cut:

• 58 small circles.

From red print, gold print, and blue print, cut:

• 13 tiny circles.

• 3 small circles.

• 5 medium circles.

• 1 large circle.

From green print, cut:

• 3 (1¼"-wide) bias strips for stems. Fold bias strips in thirds lengthwise, press, and hand baste fold in place to prepare stems for appliqué.

From binding fabric, cut:

• 4 (2¼"-wide) strips.

My Style Pillows

Marianne Fons and her daughter Mary had fun making pillows that show their differences in decorating style. Marianne's pillows have a traditional look.

25-patch Pillow

Size: 20" × 20"

MATERIALS

NOTE: Fabrics in Marianne's pillows are from the Lindsay collection by Karen Montgomery for Timeless Treasures.

5 fat quarters★★ in red print, tan print, brown solid, leaf print, and stripe
¾ yard backing fabric
20" square pillow form
★★fat quarter = 18" × 20"

Cutting

Measurements include ¼" seam allowances.

From each fat quarter, cut:
- 2 (4½") strips. From strips, cut 5 (4½") squares.

From backing fabric, cut:
- 1 (24½"-wide) strip. From strip, cut 2 (24½" × 20½") rectangles.

Pillow Top Assembly

1. Lay out squares as shown in photo on page 87 and *Pillow Top Assembly Diagram.*

2. Join into rows; join rows to complete pillow top.

Finishing

1. Fold backing rectangles in half crosswise, wrong sides facing; press.

2. Overlap pressed edges, making a square the same size as pillow top. Baste overlapped edges together *(Backing Diagram).*

3. Place pillow top atop backing, right sides facing. Stitch around outer edge, rounding corners slightly *(Stitching Diagram).*

4. Turn right side out through opening in pillow back. Insert pillow form inside pillow cover.

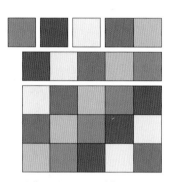

Pillow Top Assembly Diagram

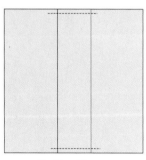

Backing Diagram

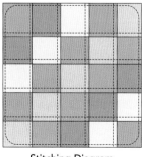

Stitching Diagram

Sawtooth Pillow

Size: 20" × 20"

MATERIALS

⅜ yard red print
1 fat quarter★★ leaf print
1 fat eighth★ beige print
1 fat eighth★ tan print
1 fat eighth★ brown solid
1 fat quarter★★ stripe
¾ yard backing fabric
21" square lining fabric
21" square batting
20" square pillow form
★fat eighth = 9" × 20"
★★fat quarter = 18" × 20"

Cutting

Measurements include ¼" seam allowances. Border strips are exact length needed. You may want to make them longer to allow for piecing variations.

From red print, cut:
- 1 (2⅞"-wide) strip. From strip, cut 8 (2⅞") squares. Cut squares in half diagonally to make 16 half-square A triangles.
- 3 (2¼"-wide) strips for binding.
- 1 (1½"-wide) strip. From strip, cut 4 (1½") C squares.

From leaf print, cut:
- 1 (8½") strip. From strip, cut 1 (8½") square.

From beige print, cut:
- 2 (2⅞"-wide) strips. From strips, cut 8 (2⅞") squares. Cut squares in half diagonally to make 16 half-square A triangles.

From tan print, cut:
- 1 (3½"-wide) strip. From strip, cut 4 (3½") D squares.
- 1 (2½"-wide) strip. From strip, cut 4 (2½") B squares.

From brown solid, cut:
- 4 (1½"-wide) strips. From strips, cut 4 (1½" × 12½") inner borders.

From stripe, cut:
- 4 (3½"-wide) strips. From strips, cut 4 (3½" x 14½") outer borders.

From backing fabric, cut:
- 1 (24½"-wide) strip. From strip, cut 2 (24½" × 20½") rectangles.

Sawtooth Pillow Top Assembly

1. Join 1 red print A triangle and 1 beige print A triangle to make a triangle-square *(Triangle-Square Diagrams)*. Make 16 triangle-squares.

Triangle-Square Diagrams

2. Referring to *Pillow Top Assembly Diagram*, lay out 4 triangle-squares. Join to make 1 Sawtooth Row. Make 4 Sawtooth Rows.

3. Add Sawtooth Rows to sides of leaf print square. Add tan print B squares to ends of remaining

Sawtooth Rows; add to top and bottom of pillow top.

4. Add brown solid inner borders to sides of pillow top. Add red print C squares to ends of remaining inner borders. Add borders to top and bottom of pillow top.

5. Add stripe outer borders to sides of pillow top. Add tan print D squares to ends of remaining outer borders. Add borders to top and bottom of pillow top.

Finishing

1. Layer lining, batting, and pillow top. Quilt in the ditch. Trim batting and lining even with edges of pillow top.

2. Fold backing fabric in half crosswise, wrong sides facing; press.

3. Overlap pressed edges, making a square the same size as pillow top. Baste overlapped edges together *(Backing Diagram on page 88)*.

4. Place pillow top atop backing, wrong sides facing. Baste around edges.

5. Join 2¼"-wide red print strips into 1 continuous piece for straight-grain French-fold binding. Add binding to pillow cover.

6. Insert pillow form inside pillow cover.

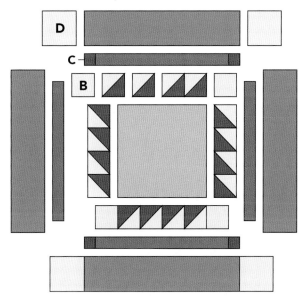

Pillow Top Assembly Diagram

My Style Pillows

Mary Fons made these easy, trendy pillows perfect for a chic apartment or loft.

Strippy Pillow

PROJECT RATING: EASY
Size: 20" × 20"

MATERIALS

NOTE: Fabrics in Mary's pillows are from the Taxi collection by Timeless Treasures.
4 fat eighths★ assorted yellow prints
4 fat eighths★ assorted black prints
¾ yard black solid for backing
20" square pillow form
★fat eighth = 9" × 20"

Cutting

Measurements include ¼" seam allowances.

From each yellow print fat eighth, cut:
• 2 (3"-wide) strips for strip sets.

From each black print fat eighth, cut:
• 2 (3"-wide) strips for strip sets.

From black solid, cut:
• 1 (24½"-wide) strip. From strip, cut 2 (24½" × 20½") rectangles.

Strippy Pillow Assembly

1. Join 4 yellow print strips and 4 black print strips alternately as shown in *Strip Set #1 Diagram*. Press seams toward bottom. From strip set #1, cut 1 (9½"-wide) segment A and 1 (7"-wide) segment B.

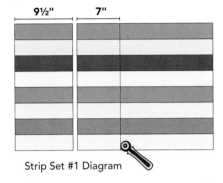

Strip Set #1 Diagram

2. Lay out remaining strips in the same order. Remove bottom strip and place it at top of layout; join strips to make Strip Set #2 as shown in *Strip Set #2 Diagram*. Press seams toward top. From strip set #2, cut 1 (5"-wide) segment C.

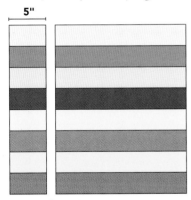

Strip Set #2 Diagram

3. Join segments A, B, and C as shown in *Pillow Top Assembly Diagram* to complete pillow top.

4. Refer to 25-Patch Pillow Finishing Instructions on page 88 to finish pillow.

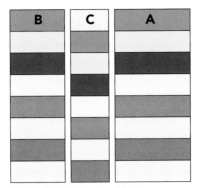

Pillow Top Assembly Diagram

Frame Pillow

PROJECT RATING: EASY

Size: 20" × 20"

MATERIALS

1 fat quarter★★ black print
1 fat eighth★ yellow print
¼ yard white print
1 yard black solid for backing
21" square lining
21" square batting
20" square pillow form
★fat eighth = 9" × 20"
★★fat quarter = 18" × 20"

Cutting

Measurements include ¼" seam allowances.

From black print, cut:
• 1 (12½") square, centering design.

From yellow print, cut:
• 4 (1½"-wide) strips. From strips, cut 2 (1½" × 14½") B rectangles and 2 (1½" × 12½") A rectangles.

From white print, cut:
• 2 (3½"-wide) strips. From strips, cut 2 (3½" × 20½") D rectangles and 2 (3½" × 14½") C rectangles.

From black solid, cut:
• 1 (24½"-wide) strip. From strip, cut 2 (24½" × 20½") rectangles.
• 3 (2¼"-wide) strips for binding.

Frame Pillow Assembly

1. Referring to *Pillow Top Assembly Diagram*, add yellow print A rectangles to sides of center square. Add yellow print B rectangles to top and bottom of pillow top.

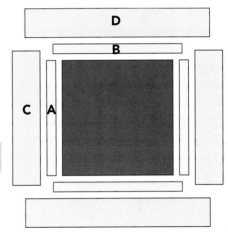

Pillow Top Assembly Diagram

2. Add white print C rectangle to sides of pillow top. Add D rectangles to top and bottom to complete pillow top.

3. Refer to Sawtooth Pillow Finishing Instructions on page 89 to finish pillow using black binding. ❋

PROJECT BY **Amy J. Martello**.

Gift Card Pockets

Amy J. Martello designed these little pockets perfect for holding gift, business, or credit cards and can be personalized for the recipient.

PROJECT RATING: EASY

Size: 4" × 2½"

MATERIALS

5" × 8" rectangle fabric for pocket
5" × 8" rectangle fabric for lining
5" × 8" rectangle thin quilt batting
Hook and loop tape
Button or ribbon flower (optional)

Cutting

Measurements include ¼" seam allowances. Patterns for pocket and optional flap designs are on pages 94–95.

From pocket fabric, lining fabric, and batting cut:

• 1 Pocket each.

Pocket Assembly

1. Layer pieces in the following order: pocket, right side up; lining right side down; and batting on top. Pin layers together.
2. Stitch around edge, leaving opening between dots as indicated. Backstitch at each dot.
3. Trim batting seam allowance close to stitching. Trim fabric seam allowance to ⅛".
4. Turn right side out; press.
5. With lining facing up, fold bottom edge up 2⅜". Press. Topstitch close to both sides to create pocket (*Stitching Diagram*).

Stitching Diagram

6. Press top flap down. Attach small piece of hook and loop tape to flap and pocket for closure. Add decorative button or ribbon flower to flap.

Optional Flap Designs

1. Make template for desired flap.
2. Align bottom of flap piece with top dashed fold line on pocket pattern when cutting out fabric piece.

Optional Contrasting Flap

1. Cut 1 (5½" × 6½") rectangle from main fabric and 1 (5½" × 2½") rectangle from contrasting fabric. Join them to make pieced rectangle; press seam open (*Pieced Rectangle Diagram*).
2. Cut pocket piece from pieced rectangle, aligning top dashed fold line on pocket pattern with seam of pieced rectangle (*Cutting Diagram*).
3. Make pocket as described in Pocket Assembly.

Pieced Rectangle Diagram

Cutting Diagram

DESIGNER

Amy J. Martello, of Ocala, Florida, draws inspiration from nature, architecture, and art. In addition to quilting, she also enjoys gardening, photography, knitting, woodworking, and making stained glass. Amy enjoys traveling with her favorite quilting friend, Sarah, to retreats and shop hops. ✳

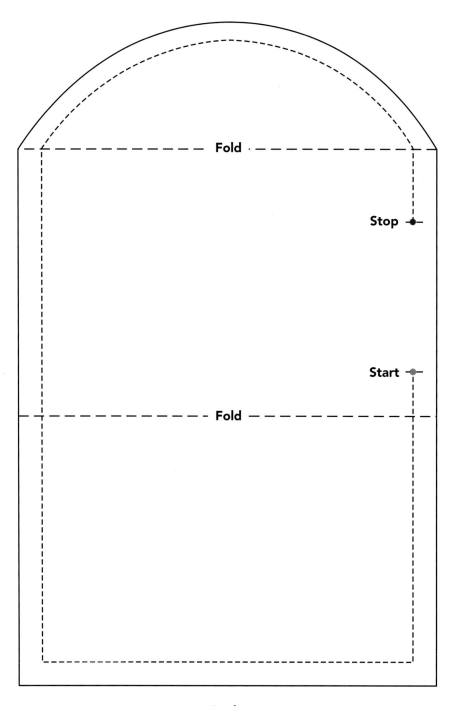

Pocket

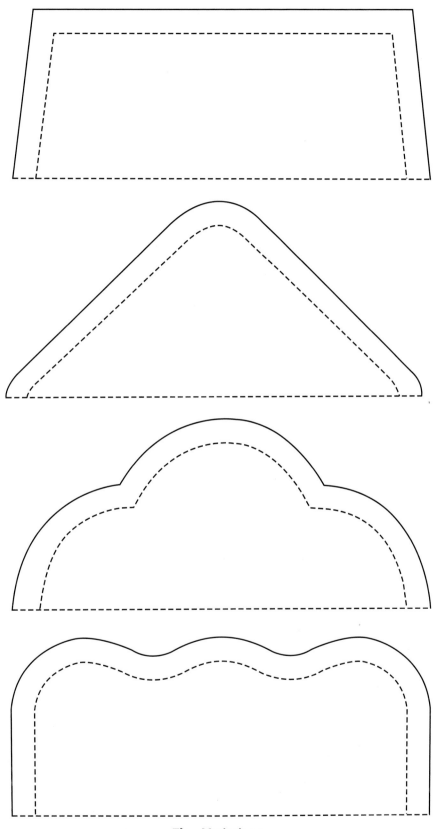

Flap Variations

PROJECT BY **Michele Wojcicki**. MADE BY **Heidi Pridemore**.

Gift Bags

Wrap up a gift in a classic fabric bag.

PROJECT RATING: EASY

Size: 4" × 15" × 4"

MATERIALS

NOTE: Fabrics in the gift bag shown are from the A Very Good Year line by Avlyn.

⅜ yard red print #1

⅛ yard red plaid print

⅜ yard red print #2

1 (4") square of heavyweight craft interfacing (optional)

Cutting

Measurements include ¼" seam allowances.

From red print #1, cut:

• 2 (4½"-wide) strips. From strips, cut 4 (4½" × 14") A rectangles for sides and 1 (4½") B square for bottom.

From red plaid print, cut:

• 1 (2"-wide) strip. From strip, cut 2 (2" × 8") D rectangles for handles and 4 (2" × 4½") C rectangles for sides.

From red print #2 print, cut:

• 2 (4½"-wide) strips. From strips, cut 4 (4½" × 15½") E rectangles and 1 (4½") B square for lining.

Bag Assembly

1. Referring to *Side Assembly Diagram*, join 1 red plaid C rectangle and 1 red print #1 A rectangle to make 1 Side Unit. Make 4 Side Units.

2. Referring to *Assembly Diagram,* join Side Units to red print #1 B bottom square.

3. Starting at the corner of bottom, stitch each side seam being careful to not catch seam allowance of bottom square in seam.

4. Repeat Steps #2 and #3 using red print #2 pieces to make bag lining. Leave a 2" opening along one side seam for turning.

5. Fold 1 red plaid D strip in half lengthwise with wrong sides facing; press fold to mark handle center. Bring long raw edges into center with wrong sides facing and press. Fold handle in half so raw edges are concealed. Topstitch close to long edges to complete 1 handle. Make 2 handles.

6. Referring to *Handle Placement Diagram*, position 1 handle on side of bag as shown, aligning raw edges. Baste handle to bag. Repeat on opposite side of bag.

7. Insert bag into bag lining, right sides facing, aligning top edges and matching side seams. Join top edges. Turn right side out through opening in lining. Whipstitch opening closed.

8. Topstitch close to top edge through all layers to complete bag.

9. Insert interfacing, if desired, to stabilize bag bottom. ✳

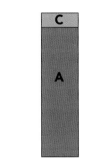

Side Assembly Diagram

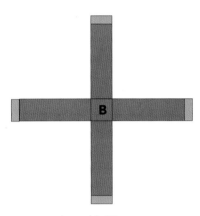

Assembly Diagram

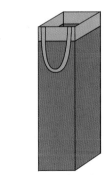

Handle Placement Diagram

Quilted Gifts

Hidden inner pockets that close with hook and look tape keep keys and other valuables secure inside the purse. Use scraps of double-faced pre-quilted fabric to make a billfold, coin purse, and tissue holder to match the purse.

PROJECT RATING: INTERMEDIATE

MATERIALS FOR ALL PROJECTS

1 yard double-faced pre-quilted fabric

1 fat quarter★ coordinating fabric for billfold pocket and binding

5" hook and loop tape

1 (7"-long) dressmaker's zipper for coin purse

1 (9"-long) dressmaker's zipper for billfold

★fat quarter = 18" × 20"

Purse

Size: 10" × 8½" × 3"

MATERIALS

¾ yard double-faced pre-quilted fabric

2 (1½"-long) pieces hook and loop tape

Cutting

Open out fabric to single thickness and cut pieces as indicated in *Cutting Diagram* on page 100.

Assembly

1. On top edge of 1 pocket, press ½" to outside. Press over ½" again to form a double hem. Machine topstitch hem. Press under ½" on sides and bottom edge of pocket. Center and sew hook side of 1 piece of hook and loop tape on wrong side of pocket just below top hem. Repeat for second pocket.

2. Stitch a ½" double hem on both short sides of purse rectangle, turning back side of fabric to front to create contrasting trim.

3. On wrong side of purse rectangle, center and stitch loop side of 1 piece of hook and loop tape down 3" from each hemmed short side.

4. Center 1 pocket at each end on wrong side of purse rectangle so sides of hook and loop tape are aligned. Topstitch pockets to purse rectangle.

5. Join handle pieces with diagonal seam as if you were making binding. Trim strip to 76" long. (If longer handles are desired, leave strip full length.) Using a diagonal seam, join ends of handle strip to form a loop. Press handle in half lengthwise, with wrong sides facing, to create center fold. Open out handle and press both edges so they meet at the center fold. Press handle in half again, concealing raw edges in fold. Machine topstitch along both edges of handle; add a line of stitching down center of handle.

6. Fold handle loop in half and mark divisions. Determine center of purse bottom by folding purse rectangle in half with hemmed edges meeting. Pin handle loop to purse rectangle so marked divisions of handle are aligned with center of purse bottom, and outside edges of handle are 3½" from sides of purse (*Purse Assembly Diagram* on page 100). Stitch handle to purse, stopping just below top hemmed edges.

7. Join sides of purse with French seam.

Sew Smart™

Sewing a French Seam

Place fabric pieces wrong sides together and join with ¼" seam. Turn wrong side out so right sides of pieces are facing and seam allowances are inside. Stitch with ½" seam that encases and conceals seam allowances. —Liz

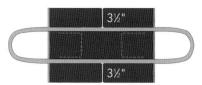

Purse Assembly Diagram

3½"

3½"

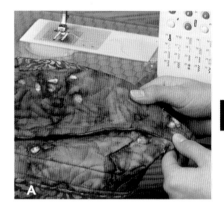

A

8. On 1 side of purse, align side seam and center of purse bottom to create a triangle. Stitch across triangle about 1½" from corner. *(See Photo A.)* Repeat for other bottom corner. Turn purse right side out. If desired, add reinforcement to purse bottom.

Tissue Holder
Size: 4½" × 2½" × 1"

MATERIALS

6" × 9" rectangle double-faced pre-quilted fabric

Assembly

1. On 1 (6"-long) side of rectangle, press ½" to outside. Press over ½" again to form a double hem. Machine topstitch hem. repeat for other 6"-long side.

2. Fold rectangle in half with finished edges meeting and mark center points with chalk or pins. With right sides facing, fold rectangle into a loop, overlapping finished edges by about ¼" to ½" at center marks. Stitch both ends with a ¼" seam.

3. On 1 side, align center of side of holder with end seam to create a triangle. Stitch across triangle about ½" from corner. Repeat for remaining corners.

4. Turn right side out through opening and place purse-size facial tissue packet inside.

Coin Purse
Size: 5" × 3¾"

MATERIALS

2 (6" × 5") rectangles pre-quilted fabric
7"-long dressmaker's zipper

Assembly

1. Zigzag or serge along all sides of both rectangles. Machine topstitch hem. Repeat for other 6"-long side.

2. Place zipper wrong side up on right side of 1 (6"-long) edge of 1 rectangle. Use zipper foot to stitch zipper to rectangle. Repeat to attach zipper to other rectangle. Open zipper about halfway; trim zipper tape even with edge of rectangle.

3. With right sides of rectangles facing, stitch sides and bottom with ½" seam.

4. Turn coin purse right side out through zipper opening.

Selvage

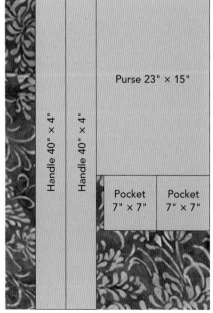

Handle 40" × 4"

Handle 40" × 4"

Purse 23" × 15"

Pocket 7" × 7"

Pocket 7" × 7"

Cutting Diagram

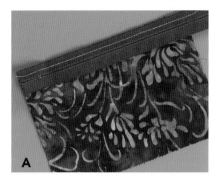

A

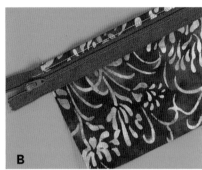

B

Billfold

Size: 7" × 4¼"

MATERIALS

7" × 12" rectangle pre-quilted fabric
1 fat quarter★ contrasting fabric for
    pocket lining and binding
9"-long dressmaker's zipper
2 (1½"-long) pieces hook and loop
    tape
★fat quarter = 18" × 20"

Assembly

1. Place zipper wrong side up on
right side of 1 (7"-long) edge of
pocket lining. Use zipper foot
to stitch zipper to pocket lining
(Photo A). Fold lining over edge
of zipper tape, encasing zipper tape
and exposing zipper teeth. Top
stitch close to fold *(Photo B)*.

2. Round off corners on 1 end of
quilted fabric to create curved
top edge. On straight lower edge,
center and sew loop side of hook
and loop tape to right side of
quilted fabric about 1¾" from
lower raw edge.

3. Stitch opposite side of zipper to
lower edge of quilted fabric. Fold
quilted fabric back, exposing zipper
teeth, and top stitch close to fold
(Photo C).

4. Press under ½" on side of pocket
lining opposite zipper. Top stitch
folded edge to wrong side of
quilted fabric. Zipper will be at
lower edge of right side of quilted
fabric. Open zipper about halfway;
trim zipper tape even with edge of
billfold.

5. Encase outer edge of quilted piece
with binding, leaving about ¾" extra
binding at each end *(Photo D)*.

6. Fold up lower edge of quilted
fabric along stitching line that
secured lower edge of pocket
lining, creating a pocket. Zipper
will be facing out. Tuck ends of
binding under and stitch sides of
pocket along edges of binding
(Photo E).

7. Fold down curved billfold top
edge to determine placement
for hook side of hook and loop
tape. Stitch tape to wrong side of
billfold flap. ✳

C

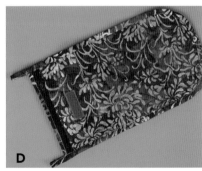

D

E

Crazy About Quilts Watchband

Fran Teagarden used fabric bits and pieces to create this clever quilted watchband.

PROJECT RATING: INTERMEDIATE

MATERIALS

10 (2") squares assorted print fabrics for piecing

6" square red print fabric for band ends and lining

6" square fusible interfacing

2" of (¾"-wide) grosgrain ribbon—cut into 2 (¾" × 1") pieces

1" of (⅝"-wide) hook-and-loop tape

Lightweight non-fusible interfacing for foundation piecing

4" × 6" piece of batting

Watch face with attachment pins

Cutting

Follow manufacturer's instructions for using fusible interfacing. Pattern pieces include ¼" seam allowances.

1. Trace band pieces A, B, C, and D onto fusible interfacing.

2. Fuse interfacing to red print fabric and cut out band pieces on drawn lines.

Pieced Block Assembly

1. Trace *Pieced Block Pattern* on page 103 onto non-fusible interfacing.

2. Using assorted print fabrics, foundation piece the block, adding pieces in numerical order. Trim edges of block on solid outside line. Make 2 pieced blocks.

Watchband Assembly

1. Join band front A to end of 1 pieced block. Fold grosgrain ribbon in half and baste raw edges to opposite end of pieced block.

2. With right sides facing, stitch band front to band lining B leaving an opening on one side. Trim, turn, press, and stitch opening closed. Quilt band.

3. Cut hook-and-loop tape to match curve of watchband; stitch loop piece to lining side of band.

4. In a similar manner, use 1 pieced block and C and D pieces to make other half of band. Stitch hook side of hook-and-loop tape to right side of band.

5. Attach watch face to band by slipping band attachment pins through ribbon loops on ends of band sections.

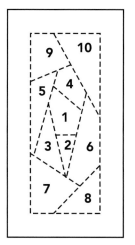

Pieced Block Pattern

TRIED & TRUE

Fran has designed several other watchbands.

Band Lining D

Band Front A

Band Front C

Band Lining B

DESIGNER

Fran Teagarden is a former home economics teacher. She has been sewing since childhood. Fran lives in Grand Junction, Iowa. ✳

PROJECT BY **Vicki Konrady**.

Chenille Scarf

With just a few quick, simple steps, you can transform a plaid flannel fabric into a cuddly chenille scarf with curly "dreadlock" fringe for everyone on your Christmas list.

PROJECT RATING: EASY
Size: 6" × 65"

NOTE: Do not prewash fabrics!

MATERIALS

NOTE: 54"–60"-wide yarn-dyed flannel fabric is easiest to use for this project because you won't need to do as much piecing. You can also use standard width flannels. Refer to *Sew Easy: Faux Chenille* on page 106 for extra supplies and tips for this technique. This project is an adaptation of the Basic Chenille Technique.

2½ yards 54"–60"-wide flannel or 3 yards 40"–45"-wide flannel
Rotary cutter and 6" × 24" ruler
Tailor's chalk

Cutting and Layering 54"–60"-wide Flannel

1. Open out fabric to full width. Fold 1 corner of fabric at a 45-degree angle to create a triangle. The folded edge will be on the bias. Using a rotary cutter and ruler, measure 4" from fold and cut a strip of fabric the length of the fold *(Cutting Diagram 1)*. You will have an 8"-wide strip of fabric cut on the bias. Remove triangle. Lay cut strip atop remaining fabric, aligning edge of strip with bias edge of fabric. Cut along edge of strip to cut another 8"-wide bias strip *(Cutting Diagram 2)*. In this manner, cut a total of 5 (8"-wide) bias strips.

2. Lay out 1 bias strip right side up. Lightly spray strip with fabric adhesive. Layer a strip atop with right side up. Repeat to make 3 layers.

3. Turn layered strips over. In a similar manner, add 2 more bias strips for a total of 5 layers.

Angled edges at ends of scarf will not match previous ones. Trim ends so they are square *(Trimming Diagram)*.

Cutting and Layering 40"–45"-wide Flannel

1. Follow instructions for Step #1 above, except keep fabric triangle in place so you cut it as you cut remaining fabric. Cut all of the fabric into 8"-wide bias strips. Some strips will be shorter.

Cutting Line

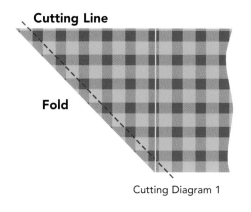

Fold

Cutting Diagram 1

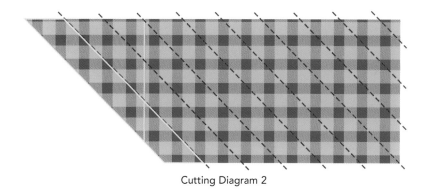

Cutting Diagram 2

Trimming Diagram

40" Layering Diagram

2. Choose 2 bias strips to join to make a strip approximately 70" long after ends are trimmed straight. Join pieces with a ¼"-wide seam. Press seam allowances open. This will be the center layer of the scarf. Lightly spray strip with fabric adhesive.

3. Layer 1 long bias strip atop center layer. Choose a shorter strip to complete the length, butting diagonal ends together *(40" Layering Diagram)*. Repeat to add a third layer, arranging butted ends so they are not atop point where ends on second layer meet. You will now have 3 layers.

4. Turn scarf over and repeat to add 2 more layers of bias strips for a total of 5 layers. Angled edges at ends of scarf will not match previous ones. Trim ends so they are square *(Trimming Diagram)*.

Assembly and Finishing

1. Mark a chalk stitching line down the length of the scarf center. Using a walking foot, stitch on marked line. Using width of walking foot as a seam guide, stitch parallel lines spaced approximately every ⅜"–½" to cover half of scarf. Turn scarf and stitch parallel lines on opposite side of center line so scarf is covered with parallel rows of stitching.

2. On sides of scarf, trim excess fabric so fabric along outside edges extends one half the width of parallel rows of stitching. For example, if rows of stitching are ½" apart, trim each long side ¼" from outer line of stitching.

3. Cut between all rows of stitching, cutting through the top 2 layers of fabric only. Turn scarf over and repeat. The middle layer will be intact.

4. Mark a chalk line 6" from each end of scarf for fringe guide. Cut through the middle fabric layer up to chalk line between all rows of stitching at both scarf ends to create fringe.

5. Machine wash and dry scarf to fluff the chenille.

Sew **Smart**™

The real fun with this project begins when you take it out of the dryer and see the exciting result—a cuddly, soft scarf with curled, fringed ends. It continues when you get compliments on this quick and easy fashion accessory. —Liz

DESIGNER

Vicki Konrady has been creating wearables for many years and has made more than 100 quilted garments for her family, close friends, and herself. She presents trunk shows and lectures to local quilt groups and teaches workshops on her wearable creations. ✳

Sew *Easy*™ Faux Chenille

Easy enough for a beginner, this fun technique will add texture to your stitching projects. Along with basic sewing supplies, you will need a pair of electric scissors or a set of narrow cutting mat strips designed for cutting chenille. You'll also need a walking foot for your sewing machine and temporary fabric adhesive spray to "baste" fabric layers. The *Chenille Scarf* on page 104 features this technique.

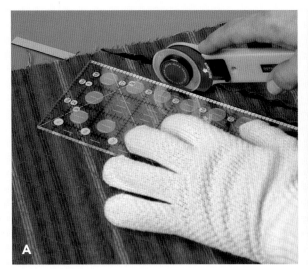

Basic Chenille Technique

Follow the steps below to create faux chenille from conventional fabric. Although any fabrics will work for this technique, flannel makes particularly snuggly chenille projects.

1. Spray right side of fabric piece with temporary fabric adhesive. Add next fabric and spray. In this manner, stack and "baste" 3–5 layers of fabric.

2. Mark a diagonal line across fabric on the bias. Using a walking foot, machine stitch along line. Using width of walking foot as a guide, stitch lines parallel to first stitching line (⅜"–¾" apart) until piece is completely stitched.

3. Cut between all rows of stitching. For most chenille projects, cut through all layers except the bottom layer. To cut using mat strips, choose a strip that fits between rows of stitching. Slip mat strip between the bottom layer and next layer. Use a ruler to guide rotary cutter as you cut. The mat strip protects the bottom fabric layer from being cut. *(Photo A)*. To cut with electric scissors, slip bottom blade of scissors between bottom fabric layer and next layer *(Photo B)*. Cut through all but the bottom fabric layer.

Sew **Smart**™
Cutting with electric scissors is fast and fun. We feel they are well worth the cost if you plan to make many chenille projects. —Liz

4. If you are making a chenille throw, finish edges with binding. Machine wash and dry project so cut edges curl.

Sew **Smart**™
Check the lint filter on your dryer frequently since it will collect lots of lint when you launder a chenille project for the first time. —Marianne

PROJECT BY **Shon McMain**.

Fleece Baby Blanket

Simple enough for a child to make, this is a baby blanket you can begin on the day the baby is born and deliver the next day. For a quick gift for an older child or adult, look for printed fleece that reflects the recipient's interests such as basketball, cars and trucks, or a northwoods theme.

PROJECT RATING: EASY
Size: 56" × 56"

MATERIALS

1¾ yards 60"-wide printed fleece

Instructions

1. Trim fleece to 56" × 56".

2. Cut out a 6" square at each corner. Fringe edge of fleece by making 6" deep cuts approximately every 2" around perimeter of fleece square.

Sew Smart™

Use a rotary cutter and ruler, or just snip in the length of your scissors blades. —Liz

3. Tie a snug knot in each piece of fringe close to inner edge of blanket.

Sew Smart™

We decorated our blanket by cutting flowers from extra fleece and machine tacking them atop flowers printed on the fleece. —Marianne

Dolly Bag

Designer Jenny Foltz made this cute doll carrier with a matching blanket, pillow, and pillowcase. They're perfect for a young girl to take her dolly with her on an adventure.

PROJECT RATING: EASY

Size: 12" × 14"

MATERIALS

NOTE: Fabrics shown are from the Sweetheart Ballerinas collection by Phyllis Dobbs for Quilting Treasures.

1½ yards pink stripe

1 yard aqua print

¾ yard white print

Crib-size quilt batting

1 (⅝"-diameter) white button

Cutting

Measurements include ¼" seam allowances. Scallop pattern is on page 110.

From pink stripe, cut:

- 1 (18"-wide) strip. From strip, cut 2 (18") squares for blanket.
- 1 (12"-wide) strip. From strip, cut 2 (12" × 2") rectangles for bag handles, 1 (9") square for bag pocket flap, and 1 (9" × 3") rectangle for pillow case trim.
- 80" of 2¼"-wide bias strips. Join strips to make bias binding for bag.

From aqua print, cut:

- 1 (20"-wide) strip for bag pieces.
- 1 (7"-wide) strip. From strip, cut 1 (7" × 9") rectangle for pillow case and 2 (2" × 12") rectangles for bag handles.

From white print, cut:

- 1 (20"-wide) strip for bag pieces.
- 1 (4½"-wide) strip. From strip, cut 1 (4½" × 14") rectangle for pillow.

From batting, cut:

- 1 (20" × 40") piece for bag pieces.
- 2 (11" × 2") rectangles for bag handles.

Dolly Bag Assembly

1. Layer 20"-wide strip of white print, wrong side up, 20" × 40" piece of batting, and 20"-wide strip of aqua print, right side up; baste. Quilt through all layers with parallel diagonal lines 1" apart. From quilted fabric, cut pieces as indicated in *Cutting Diagram.*

2. Mark scallops on front and back pieces, evenly spacing scallops. Cut pieces on marked line.

3. Zigzag or serge around sides and bottom of pocket piece to finish edges.

4. Layer 1 (2" × 11") batting rectangle; 1 (2" × 12") pink stripe rectangle, right side up; and 1 (2" × 12") aqua print rectangle, right side down. Fabric strips are ½" longer than batting at each end. Sew long sides of layered rectangles. Turn right side out; press. Topstitch ½" from long edges and through middle. Repeat to make second handle.

5. Fold pink print pocket flap square in half diagonally, right sides facing. Stitch edges together, leaving an opening for turning. Turn right side out, press. Topstitch close to edges to make pocket flap.

6. Place pocket flap atop aqua print side of pocket rectangle. Stitch pocket flap to top of pocket rectangle, as shown in *Pocket Diagrams* on page 110. Press pocket flap to white print side of pocket. Topstitch ¼" from top edge of pocket. Sew button to pocket flap.

7. Press under ½" on sides and bottom of pocket. Center and pin pocket to right side of bag front, 1¼" up from bottom, as shown in *Bag Assembly Diagram* on page 110. Topstitch pocket to bag front.

8. Add binding to top scalloped edge of bag front. Repeat for bag back.

9. Fold top of bag front to right side, 2¼" from top. Repeat for bag back.

10. Position 1 handle on front of bag as shown. Fold ends under ¼" and topstitch through all layers to

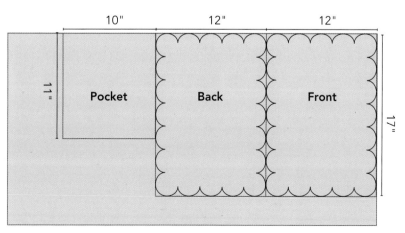

Cutting Diagram

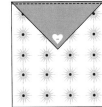

Pocket Diagrams

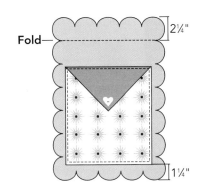
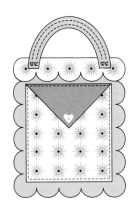

Fold—

2¼"

1¼"

Bag Assembly Diagrams

attach handle to bag. Repeat for bag back.

11. Place bag front atop bag back, wrong sides facing; stitch along sides and bottom scalloped edges. Add binding to sides and bottom scalloped edges.

Pillow/Pillowcase Assembly

1. Fold white print pillow rectangle in half, right sides facing. Stitch with a ½" seam, leaving a small opening for turning. Turn right side out.

2. Stuff pillow with fiberfill. Stitch opening closed.

3. Fold pink stripe pillowcase trim rectangle in half along long side, wrong sides facing. Join pillowcase trim to aqua print pillowcase rectangle.

4. Fold pillowcase in half, right sides facing. Stitch side and bottom seams. Turn right side out. Press. Insert pillow into pillowcase.

Blanket Assembly

With right sides facing, stitch pink stripe blanket squares together, leaving a small opening for turning. Turn right side out. Press. Topstitch close to edges.

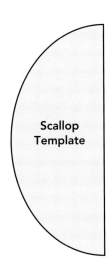

Scallop Template

DESIGNER

When Jenny was a little girl, her mother always encouraged her creativity and imagination. Her inspiration for designing fun and fresh quilt patterns at her company, Jenny Foltz Quilt Design, comes from her love of art and the freedom to dream, create, and discover. With so much in her life as inspiration, most importantly her sons and her passion for art, she will continue to develop quilts that reflect this love and appreciation. ✳

Coloring Apron

Little artists will enjoy this child's coloring apron which holds 24 crayons in divided pockets.

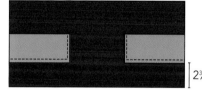

2¾"

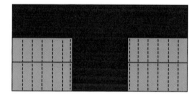

Pocket Stitching Diagrams

PROJECT RATING: EASY

Size: Age 3–4 and 5–6

MATERIALS

½ yard pink print for apron

¼ yard green print for pockets

24 crayons

Cutting

NOTE: Instructions are written for small size age 3–4. Instructions in blue are for age 5–6.

From pink print, cut:

• 2 (9" × 19") (11" × 20") rectangles for apron front and lining.

• 1 (2½" × 36") (2½" × 40") strips for waistband and ties.

From green print, cut:

• 4 (6" × 7") rectangles for pockets.

Apron Assembly

1. Fold 1 pocket rectangle in half, right sides facing, and 7"-long edges aligned; press. Stitch along 1 (3"-long) edge, ½" from edge *(Pocket Stitching Diagrams)*. Turn right side out; press. Make 4 pocket sections.

Sew **Smart**™

If using directional fabric for the pockets, sew along right edge of 2 pocket sections and left edge of 2 pocket sections. —Liz

2. Pin 2 pocket sections to apron front 2¾" from bottom edge and with outer raw edges aligned. Topstitch close to 3" edge and ¼" from bottom edge as shown.

3. Pin remaining 2 pocket sections to apron front, overlapping upper pocket section ¼" and aligning bottom and outer edges.

4. Topstitch through all layers close to inner edge and at 1" intervals, creating 6 sections for crayons in each pocket. Backstitch at each end to reinforce stitching.

5. Place apron front atop lining, right sides facing. Stitch along sides and bottom with a ½" seam allowance. Turn apron right side out; press.

6. Sew 2 rows of basting stitches ⅛" and ⅜" from top edge of apron. Pull bobbin threads to gather top edge of apron to 12" (14"). Adjust gathers evenly.

7. Referring to *Waistband Diagrams,* center and pin apron to waistband, right sides facing. Stitch apron to waistband.

8. Fold waistband in half lengthwise, wrong side out. Keeping apron free, stitch waistband ties using a ¼" seam allowance, stopping at the edges of apron. Turn ties right side out. Press seam allowance of waistband on wrong side of apron to inside. Topstitch close to edges of entire waistband and ties.

9. Fill pockets with crayons.

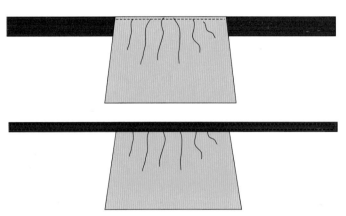

Waistband Diagrams

DESIGNER

After many years of working at a community college, Evonne Cook opened a quilt shop with her best friend. They later sold the shop, but Evonne markets her patterns through her company, Clothesline Quilts. www.clotheslinequilts.com ❋

Groovy Backpack

This totally cool backpack from pre-quilted fabric is fun to make and is perfect for a trip to the shopping mall or for toting dance shoes and practice clothes.

PROJECT RATING: INTERMEDIATE

Size: 16" × 19" × 3"

MATERIALS

1¼ yards pre-quilted fabric

⅜ yard trim fabric

1 (5"-long) piece of hook and loop tape

Cutting

From pre-quilted fabric, cut:

• Pieces as shown in *Cutting Diagram*.

From trim fabric, cut:

• 2 (17" × 5") rectangles for bottom trim.

• 1 (9" × 7") rectangle for pocket flap trim.

Assembly

1. Press under ½" along 1 long side of each 17" × 5" trim rectangle.

2. On right side of front piece, pin prepared trim strip to lower edge, aligning raw edges *(Assembly Diagram)*. Topstitch folded edge of trim to bag. Repeat for back piece.

3. Zigzag stitch or serge around front, back, and pocket pieces to finish edges.

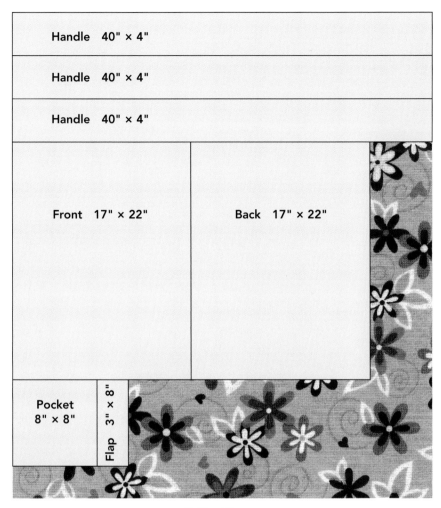

Cutting Diagram

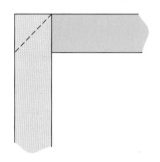

Assembly Diagram

Diagonal Seam Diagram

4. Cut 1 handle strip in half to make 2 (4" × 20") pieces. Using diagonal seam, join 1 short handle piece to 1 long handle piece *(Diagonal Seam Diagram)*. Press handle in half lengthwise, with wrong sides facing, to create center fold. Open out handle and press both edges so they meet at the center fold. Press handle in half again, concealing raw edges in fold. Machine topstitch along both edges of handle; add a line of stitching down center of handle. Repeat to make second handle.

5. Stitch a ½" double-fold hem along top edge of pocket square.

On right side of pocket, center and sew loop side of hook and loop tape 1" below hemmed top edge of pocket. Press under ½" on remaining edges of pocket.

6. Fold flap trim rectangle in half, wrong sides facing, and press fold to mark center; open out fold. Center and sew hook side of hook and loop tape to right side of flap trim ½" above center fold.

7. Fold flap trim strip in half with right sides facing. Baste sides with ½" seam allowance; turn right side out and press. Slip 3" × 8" pre-quilted pocket flap rectangle inside prepared trim and check

fit. Remove pre-quilted piece and stitch sides of trim, adjusting seam width as needed for a good fit. Turn prepared trim right side out, insert pre-quilted flap piece, and top stitch ⅛" from sides and folded edge. Press under raw edges of flap ½".

8. Center and pin prepared pocket to right side of bag front with bottom edge of pocket 7" above lower edge. Sew pocket to backpack front piece, stitching ⅛" from sides and bottom.

9. Pin pocket flap above pocket. Topstitch along folded edge to attach flap to front piece.

A

B

catching handle ends in side seams *(Photo B)*.

16. Align side seam and bottom seam to create a triangle. Stitch across triangle about 1½" from corner *(Photo C)*.

17. Turn backpack right side out. To close top of backpack, pull on handle pairs on each side. ✻

10. With right sides facing, pin front piece to back piece. Taking a ½" seam, sew partial side seam on 1 side of backpack, beginning seam 6" down from top edge and ending seam 3" up from top edge of bottom trim.

11. Press under seam allowance toward wrong side of front piece at top of side; stitch seam allowance to front piece to finish edge. Repeat for other seam allowance.

12. Sew partial side seam on other side, fold under and finish top side seam allowances.

13. Turn under 2¼" to wrong side at top edge of front piece to form a casing for handle. Stitch ¼" from raw edge to complete casing. Repeat for back piece.

NOTE: Inserting the handles is a bit tricky. Be sure to read through the instructions before beginning.

14. Turn backpack right side out. Working from left to right, insert 1 handle through casing on front; bring same end of handle through casing on back from right to left. Both ends of handle will come out of casings on left side of backpack and handle will form a loop on right side of backpack *(Photo A)*. Repeat for other handle, bringing both ends out on right side and creating a loop on left side.

15. Turn backpack wrong side out. Pin ends of handles to sides just above top edge of lower trim. Sew side seams and bottom seam,

Wrap It to go

Dress up a plain notebook and make writing fun!
Whether you use pre-quilted fabric or quilt your own, this is
a super-quick project.

PROJECT RATING: EASY

Size: fits 7" × 9½" notebook

MATERIALS

NOTE: Pre-quilted fabric shown is from the Christmas Past collection by Minick and Simpson for Moda.

⅜ yard pre-quilted fabric

½ yard contrasting fabric for lining and binding

1" piece of hook and loop tape

1 (1⅛"-diameter) button

7" × 9½" spiral-bound notebook

Cutting

Measurements include ¼" seam allowances. If using pre-quilted fabric, cut exact sizes. If quilting your own fabrics, add 1" to measurements to allow for shrinkage during quilting. Trim to proper size after quilting.

From pre-quilted fabric, cut:

- 1 (20" × 10½") rectangle.
- 1 (5¼" × 10½") wide flap.
- 1 (3" × 10½") narrow flap.
- 1 (4" × 5") pen pocket.

From contrasting fabric, cut:

- 1 (3" × 10½") narrow flap lining.
- 1 (4" × 5") pen pocket lining.
- (2½"-wide) bias strips. Join strips to make about 72" of bias for binding.

Assembly

1. Bind one long edge of wide flap.
2. Place pen pocket atop pen pocket lining, right sides facing. Stitch around edge, leaving opening for turning. Clip corners, turn right side out, and press. Topstitch top edge of pen pocket.
3. Pin pen pocket to center of wide flap, 2¼" from bottom edge, keeping bound edge of flap to the right. Topstitch side and bottom edges of pen pocket, reinforcing stitching at top edge. Stitch through center of pen pocket to divide into 2 sections (*Wide Flap Diagram* on page 119).
4. Place narrow flap rectangle atop narrow flap lining rectangle, right sides facing; stitch both long edges. Turn right side out; press. Topstitch close to folded edges.
5. Trim one end of large quilted rectangle, rounding corners as shown in *Trimming Diagram* on page 119.
6. Referring to *Flap Placement Diagram* on page 119, pin wide flap, right side up on wrong side of large rectangle matching left edges. Pin narrow flap to large rectangle 5" from edge of wide flap. Baste flaps in place.
7. Add binding to notebook cover.

CUSTOM SIZES

With a few simple measurements you can create a cover for any size book. First, determine these 3 measurements:

Height (H) _____ **Width (W)** _____ **Thickness (T)** _____

Cutting for Rectangle Long Side: $(2\frac{1}{2} \times \underline{}) + (2 \times \underline{}) = $ _____

Cutting for Rectangle Short Side: $\underline{} + 1" = $ _____

Cutting for Wide Flap Short Side: $(\frac{1}{2} \times \underline{}) + 1" = $ _____

Cutting for Wide Flap Long Side: $\underline{} + 1" = $ _____

Length of Binding: _____ + _____ + 12" = _____
Measure perimeter of rectangle   Short side of rectangle

Placement of Narrow Flap: Measure finished width of wide flap. Position narrow flap this distance from finished edge of wide flap.

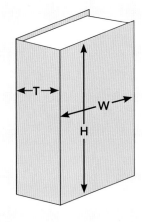

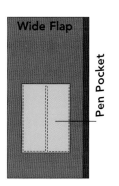

Wide Flap Diagram

Trimming Diagram

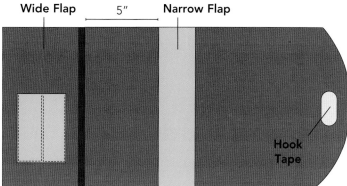

Flap Placement Diagram

8. Position loop side of hook and loop tape ½" from edge of notebook cover on inside. Stitch in place.

9. Slide front cover of notebook under wide flap and back cover under narrow flap. Close cover, fold right side into position and mark position for hook side of tape on cover front. Remove notebook and sew tape in place. Reinsert notebook.

10. Sew button to flap, covering loop tape stitching.

Sew Smart™

Trim corners of hook and loop tape in a gentle curve to eliminate sharp points. —Liz

DESIGNER

Terry Albers began writing patterns for her students while teaching at her sister's quilt shop. She now has a line of patterns and has authored three books with her friend Pam Puyleart of Cottage Creek Quilts.

www.hedgehogquilts.com

TRIED & TRUE

Personalize a notebook cover with your favorite colors. For this version, we chose fabrics from the Jasmine collection by Pamela Mostek for Clothworks. ✳

Buttons & Bows

Delight a young lady with this bright, snuggly coverlet made from textured faux fur in her favorite colors. Big buttons, tied on with lengths of ribbon, keep the layers aligned.

PROJECT RATING: EASY

Size: 70" × 90"

MATERIALS

NOTE: Yardage requirements are based on 60"-wide fabric. Fabrics in the quilt shown are from the Luscious collection by Springs.

1 yard each yellow, orange, green, blue, purple, and pink faux fur

18 yards 21"-wide lightweight fusible interfacing

63 (1⅜"-diameter) buttons in yellow, orange, green, blue, purple, and pink

Large-eye needle

5½ yards each ¼"-wide satin ribbon in yellow, orange, green, blue, purple, and pink

5½ yards 45"-wide backing fabric

Full-size quilt batting (optional)

✂ **NOTE:** The buttons on this quilt may present a choking hazard for small children.

Cutting

Measurements include ¼" seam allowances. Follow manufacturer's instructions for using fusible interfacing.

> ### Sew **Smart**™
> Fuse interfacing to wrong side of faux fur before cutting. —Liz

From each color of faux fur, cut:
- 3 (10½"-wide) strips. From strips, cut 11 (10½") squares.

Quilt Assembly

1. Lay out squares as shown in photo above. You will have a few extra squares.

2. Join into rows; join rows to complete quilt top.

> ### Sew **Smart**™
> Join 4 extra fur squares to make a 20"-square pillow top. —Liz

Finishing

1. Divide backing fabric into 2 (2¾-yard) pieces. Join panels lengthwise, leaving a 12"–14" opening in center of seam for turning.

2. Place quilt top atop backing, right sides facing. Stitch around entire outer edge of top with ¼" seam. If desired, place quilt atop batting, backing side up; pin or baste in place. From backing side, stitch around outer edge of quilt on previous stitching line through all 3 layers. Trim batting and backing even with quilt top.

3. Turn quilt right side out through opening in backing center seam. Whipstitch opening closed.

4. Sew 1 button in the center of each square through all layers. Using a large-eye needle, thread 1 (18"-long) piece of ribbon through holes in button and tie in a bow.

TRIED & TRUE

Use fleece in primary colors for a more masculine version. Machine stitch a 1½"-wide strip of fleece to each square; tie in a knot. ✳

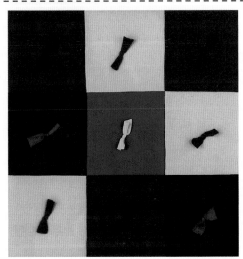

Pillowcase

If you'd like to introduce a child to machine sewing, this is a great beginner project. Kids enjoy making a pillowcase to match their bed, to carry on sleepovers, or to take to camp. To make a memory project, replace the novelty print with a light color so kids can have their friends sign it.

PROJECT RATING: EASY

Size: 21" × 30"

(fits a standard bed pillow)

MATERIALS

¾ yard novelty or theme fabric

¼ yard contrasting fabric for band

Assembly

1. If necessary, trim contrasting fabric for band so it is straight and 8½"–9" wide. Trim pillow case fabric so edges are straight and piece is approximately 27" long.

2. Fold contrasting band fabric in half with wrong sides facing so that strip is approximately 4½" wide. Press.

3. Referring to *Diagram 1*, pin contrasting band to right side of pillowcase fabric with right sides facing and raw edges aligned. Stitch with a ½" seam. Press seam allowances toward pillowcase.

Diagram 1

4. Topstitch through all layers ¼" from seam. Trim pillowcase and band as needed so that they are same width, as shown in *Diagram 2*.

Diagram 2   Diagram 3

5. Referring to *Diagram 3*, fold into a rectangle with right sides facing. Stitch along top and side edge with ½" seam.

6. Turn pillowcase right side out and press.

Sew **Smart**™
To help prevent raveling during washings, zigzag, pink, or serge raw edges of seams.
—Marianne ✳

Flannel Brick Road

Make this cozy, masculine quilt for the special guy in your life. Set aside a stack of fat quarters and a weekend and you'll be able to delight him on Christmas morning or his next birthday.

PROJECT RATING: EASY

Size: 72" × 84"

MATERIALS

NOTE: Fabrics in the quilt shown are from the Woolies II Flannel collection by Maywood Studio.

24 fat quarters★ assorted blue, red, gold, brown, and black print flannel (If you prewash your fabric, you may need a few extra fat quarters.)

¾ yard red print flannel for binding

5 yards backing fabric

Full-size quilt batting

★fat quarter = 18" × 20"

Cutting

Measurements include ¼" seam allowances.

From each fat quarter, cut:
• 5 (3½" × 20") strips. From strips, cut 15 (3½" × 6½") rectangles. You will have a few extra.

From red print, cut:
• 9 (2½"-wide) strips for binding.

Quilt Assembly

1. Referring to *Quilt Top Assembly Diagram* on page 126, join 14 rectangles to complete Row 1. Make 12 Row 1.
2. In same manner, join 15 rectangles for Row 2. Make 12 Row 2.
3. Lay out the rows, offsetting them as shown in *Quilt Top Assembly Diagram*. Join rows.
4. Trim top and bottom of quilt as shown.

Finishing

1. Divide backing into 2 (2½-yard) pieces. Divide 1 piece in half lengthwise to make 2 narrow panels. Join 1 narrow panel to each side of wider panel. Press seam allowances toward narrow panels.
2. Layer backing, batting, and quilt top; baste. Quilt as desired. Quilt shown was quilted with an X in each rectangle *(Quilting Diagram)*.
3. Join 2½"-wide red print strips into 1 continuous piece for straight-grain French-fold binding. Add binding to quilt.

Sew **Smart**™

When joining the rows of this quilt, fold every third or fourth brick in half and match fold to seam on adjoining row. —Liz

When working with flannel fabrics which are thicker than the cottons we use for most of our quilts, pressing seams open rather than to one side will help make the quilt top nice and smooth. —Marianne

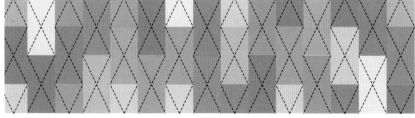

Quilting Diagram

Row 1 Row 2 Crib Throw Full Queen

Quilt Top Assembly Diagram

TRIED & TRUE

Make a fun bright version of this quilt for a child using fabrics with favorite motifs. Fabrics shown here are from the Granny's Sweete Shoppe collection by Mary Anne Henderson and the Bubbles collection by Ro Gregg for Northcott. ✳

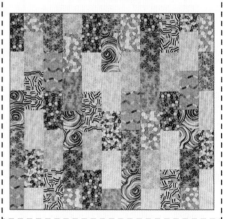

SIZE OPTIONS

Materials

	Crib (36" × 48")	Full (81" × 96")	Queen (87" × 102")
Blocks	102 rectangles	445 rectangles	507 rectangles
Setting	6 Row 1—8 rectangles	14 Row 1—16 rectangles	15 Row 1—17 rectangles
	6 Row 2—9 rectangles	13 Row 2—17 rectangles	14 Row 2—18 rectangles
Assorted Prints	7 fat quarters	30 fat quarters	34 fat quarters
Binding	½ yard	¾ yard	⅞ yard
Backing Fabric	1½ yards	7½ yards	8 yards
Batting	Crib-size	Queen-size	Queen-size
Cutting			
Each Fat Quarter	15 (3½" × 6½") rectangles	15 (3½" × 6½") rectangles	15 (3½" × 6½") rectangles

Friends Forever

Glenna Claybaugh Denman made this Friendship Star
quilt for her friend Elizabeth Page Shoemaker. She
included a photo of the girlhood friends on the label.

PROJECT RATING: EASY

Size: 58" × 70"

Blocks: 20 (12") Friendship Star Block

MATERIALS

½ yard each of 4 assorted medium/ dark blue prints for blocks

2 yards white print for blocks and inner border

1¼ yards medium blue print for blocks and outer border

⅝ yard light blue print for blocks

⅝ yard navy print for binding

Fons & Porter Half & Quarter Ruler (optional)

3¾ yards backing fabric

Twin-size quilt batting

Cutting

Measurements include ¼" seam allowances. Border strips are exact length needed. You may want to make them longer to allow for piecing variations.

To cut triangles for triangle-squares using the Fons & Porter Half & Quarter Ruler, see *Sew Easy: Cutting Half-Square Triangles* on page 131. If you are not using the Fons & Porter Half & Quarter Ruler, use the cutting **NOTE** instructions given here.

From each medium/dark blue print, cut:

• 3 (4½"-wide) strips. From strips, cut 5 (4½") A squares and 20 half-square B triangles.

NOTE: If NOT using the Fons & Porter Half & Quarter Ruler to cut the B triangles, cut 2 (4⅞"-wide) strips. From strips, cut 10 (4⅞") squares. Cut squares in half diagonally to make 20 half-square B triangles.

From white print, cut:

• 12 (4½"-wide) strips. From strips, cut 160 half-square B triangles.

NOTE: If NOT using the Fons & Porter Half & Quarter Ruler to cut the B triangles, cut 10 (4⅞"-wide) strips. From strips, cut 80 (4⅞") squares. Cut squares in half diagonally to make 160 half-square B triangles.

• 6 (2"-wide) strips. Piece strips to make 2 (2" × 51½") top and bottom inner borders and 2 (2" × 60½") side inner borders.

From medium blue print, cut:

• 3 (4½"-wide) strips. From strips, cut 32 half-square B triangles.

NOTE: If NOT using the Fons & Porter Half & Quarter Ruler to cut the B triangles, cut 2 (4⅞"-wide) strips. From strips, cut 16 (4⅞") squares. Cut squares in half diagonally to make 32 half-square B triangles.

• 7 (4"-wide) strips. Piece strips to make 2 (4" × 58½") top and bottom outer borders and 2 (4" × 63½") side outer borders.

From light blue print, cut:

• 4 (4½"-wide) strips. From strips, cut 48 half-square B triangles.

NOTE: If NOT using the Fons & Porter Half & Quarter Ruler to cut the B triangles, cut 3

(4⅞"-wide) strips. From strips, cut 24 (4⅞") squares. Cut squares in half diagonally to make 48 half-square B triangles.

From navy print, cut:

• 7 (2¼"-wide) strips for binding.

Block Assembly

1. Join 1 white print B triangle and 1 blue print B triangle to make a triangle-square *(Triangle-Square Diagrams)*. Make 160 triangle-squares.

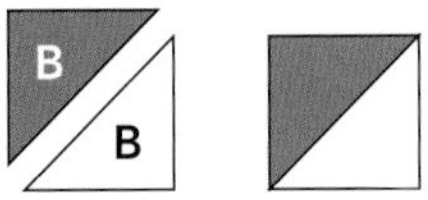

Triangle-Square Diagrams

2. Choose 1 set of 4 matching medium/dark blue triangle-squares and 1 medium/dark blue A square, and 4 matching medium blue triangle-squares.

3. Lay out triangle-squares and A square as shown in *Block Assembly Diagram*. Join into rows; join rows to complete 1 Friendship Star block *(Block Diagram)*. Make 20 blocks.

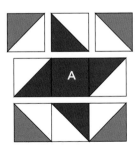

Block Assembly Diagram

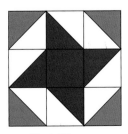

Block Diagram

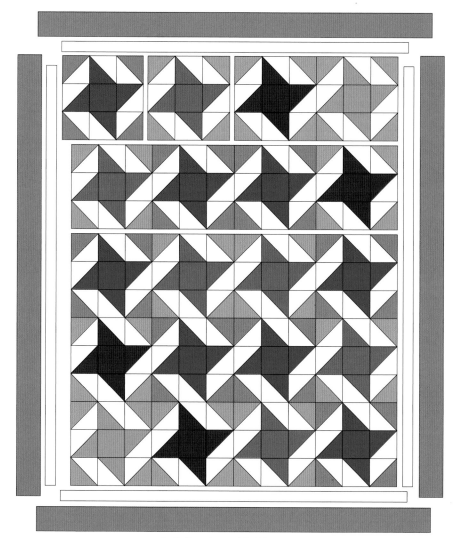

Quilt Top Assembly Diagram

Quilting Diagram

Quilt Assembly

1. Lay out blocks as shown in *Quilt Top Assembly Diagram*. Join into rows; join rows to complete quilt center.

2. Add white print side inner borders to quilt center. Add white print top and bottom inner borders to quilt.

3. Repeat for medium blue print outer borders.

Finishing

1. Divide backing into 2 (1⅞-yard) lengths. Join panels lengthwise. Seam will run horizontally.

2. Layer backing, batting, and quilt top; baste. Quilt as desired. Quilt shown was quilted in the ditch, with heart designs in the blocks, and loops in outer border *(Quilting Diagram)*.

3. Join 2¼"-wide navy print strips into 1 continuous piece for straight-grain French-fold binding. Add binding to quilt.

TRIED & TRUE

We fussy cut the center square in our bright, springy block. Fabrics shown are from the California Dreamin' collection by Jenean Morrison for FreeSpirit.

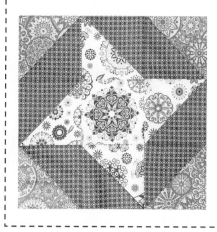

Glenna stitched a photo of the girlhood friends on the back of her quilt next to the label.

DESIGNER

Glenna Claybaugh Denman has always admired quilts, but didn't make one until her retirement in 2001. With a desire to present baby quilts to her new grandchildren, she joined a guild and began taking classes. Glenna says she is so grateful to the quilters in her guild for their warm welcome that she now loves to welcome new quilters in return. She lives in Texas, and also enjoys gardening and reading. ✳

Cutting Half-Square Triangles

Easily cut half-square triangles from strips of the same width
with the Fons & Porter Half & Quarter Ruler.

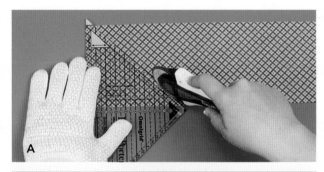

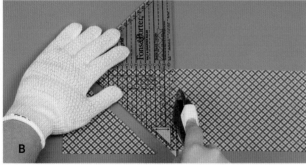

Cutting Half-Square Triangles

1. Straighten the left edge of 4½"-wide fabric strip.
   Place the 4½" line of the Fons & Porter Half &
   Quarter Ruler on the bottom edge of strip, aligning
   left edge of ruler with straightened edge of strip.
   The yellow tip of ruler will extend beyond top edge
   of strip.
2. Cut along right edge of ruler to make 1 half-square
   triangle *(Photo A)*.
3. Turn ruler and align 4½" line with top edge of strip.
   Cut along right edge of ruler *(Photo B)*.
4. Repeat to cut required number of half-square
   triangles.

MADE BY **Jean Nolte**.

My Little House

Love of Quilting Editor Jean Nolte designed this fun take-along punch needle project. Make one for yourself and another for someone on your holiday gift list.

PROJECT RATING: EASY

Size: 4" × 4"

MATERIALS

10" square weaver's cloth

2 skeins dark red embroidery floss DMC color #777

1 skein each DMC embroidery floss in light red #321, medium blue #826, dark blue #336, light gold #725, dark gold #782, and cream #3033

Fons & Porter Punch Needle

Fons & Porter Transfer Pencil

8" embroidery hoop

Instructions

1. Use transfer pencil to trace design onto paper. Center paper on fabric with transfer side down. Press paper to transfer design.

NOTE: Design will be reversed when transferred. Press according to package directions. Before moving paper, check to be sure design has transferred.

2. Stretch fabric tightly in hoop. Using 3 strands of embroidery floss, thread the punch needle according to package directions. Use the #1 or shortest punch needle loop setting.

3. Work from the design side of fabric; unprinted side is right side. Begin by punching the outline of a shape. Stitches should be done approximately 1 needle-width apart. Follow along next to the lines, filling in the space.

4. After punching the central design, punch the background and borders.

5. Working from right side, use the needle to move and rake thread loops into position so details of design are distinct.

6. Frame as desired.

> **Sew Smart**™
>
> **After completing a section, you may need to go back and fill in some areas.** —Liz ✳

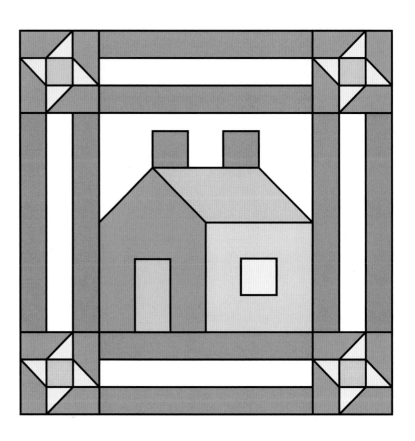

Rickrack Runner

Add a splash of color to your dining room table with this table runner by the sisters at Tailormade by Design.

PROJECT RATING: EASY
Size: 19" × 51"
Blocks: 3 (16") blocks

MATERIALS

NOTE: Fabrics in the table runner shown are from the Contemporary Charm collection by Windham Fabrics.

¼ yard purple print
½ yard purple floral
½ yard purple stripe
½ yard pink print
1 fat eighth★ pink floral
1 fat eighth★ pink stripe
3½ yards ½"-wide white rickrack
1¼ yards backing fabric
Crib-size quilt batting
★fat eighth = 9" × 20"

Cutting

Measurements include ¼" seam allowances. Border strips are exact length needed. You may want to make them longer to allow for piecing variations.

From purple print, cut:
- 2 (3½"-wide) strips. From strips, cut 2 (3½" × 16½") E rectangles, 2 (3½" × 10½") D rectangles, and 4 (3½") A squares.

From purple floral, cut:
- 1 (3½"-wide) strip. From strip, cut 4 (3½") A squares.
- 4 (2¼"-wide) strips for binding.

From purple stripe, cut:
- 1 (3½"-wide) strip. From strip, cut 5 (3½") A squares.
- 4 (2"-wide) strips. From 1 strip, cut 2 (2" × 19½") top and bottom borders. Piece remaining strips to make 2 (2" × 48½") side borders.

- 3 (1"-wide) strips. From strips, cut 4 (1" × 10½") C rectangles and 4 (1" × 9½") B rectangles.

From pink print, cut:

- 4 (3½"-wide) strips. From strips, cut 4 (3½" × 16½") E rectangles, 4 (3½" × 10½") D rectangles, and 5 (3½") A squares.

From pink floral, cut:

- 1 (3½"-wide) strip. From strip, cut 5 (3½") A squares.

From pink stripe, cut:

- 4 (3½") A squares.
- 3 (1"-wide) strips. From strips, cut 2 (1" × 10½") C rectangles and 2 (1" × 9½") B rectangles.

Block Assembly

1. Lay out 9 assorted A squares as shown in *Block Center Diagrams*. Join into rows; join rows to complete 1 block center. Make 3 block centers.

Block Center Diagrams

2. Referring to *Block Assembly Diagram*, add purple stripe B rectangles to top and bottom of block center. Add purple print C rectangles to sides of block. Repeat

for pink print D and E rectangles to complete 1 pink block *(Block Diagram)*. Make 2 pink blocks.

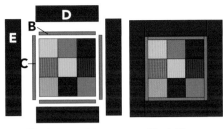

Block Assembly Diagram   Block Diagram

3. In the same manner, make 1 purple block using pink stripe B and C rectangles and purple print D and E rectangles.

4. Referring to photo, hand stitch rickrack on each block, covering seams as shown.

Table Runner Assembly

1. Lay out blocks as shown in *Assembly Diagram*. Join blocks to complete table runner center.

2. Add purple stripe top and bottom borders to table runner. Add purple stripe side borders to table runner.

Finishing

1. Divide backing into 2 (⅝-yard) lengths. Join panels end to end.

2. Layer backing, batting, and table runner top; baste. Quilt as desired. Table runner shown was quilted with a floral wreath in center of each block, in the ditch around the rectangles, and with meandering in borders *(Quilting Diagram)*.

3. Join 2¼"-wide purple floral strips into 1 continuous piece for straight-grain French-fold binding. Add binding to quilt.

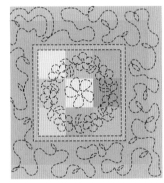

Quilting Diagram

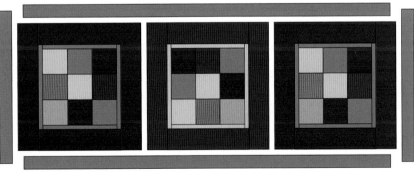

Assembly Diagram

DESIGNER

Sisters Joanie Holton and Melanie Greseth have been sewing since they were young girls. Together, they started their sewing business, Tailormade by Design, and their online quilt shop. The sisters say, "A business that allows you to be creative every day, work with your best friend, and have a huge stash of fabric is really the best job in the world." ❋

Coiled Fabric Bowls

PROJECT RATING: EASY

MATERIALS

½ yard fabric

50 feet cotton clothesline

1 snap-type clothespin

Size 100/16 sewing machine needle

Open-toe or clear plastic machine presser foot

Variegated thread such as Sulky® Blendables (30 wt) to coordinate with fabric

Cutting

From fabric, cut:

- 1"-wide strips. Exact number needed will depend on size of bowl.

Bowl Assembly

1. Fit sewing machine with size 100/16 needle. Thread sewing machine with matching thread on top and in bobbin. Choose a wide regular or multi-stitch zigzag stitch and medium stitch length. Adjust presser foot pressure to a light setting.

2. Fold about 1½" of fabric strip over freshly cut end of clothesline (Photo A). Begin wrapping fabric strip around folded fabric to secure end.

3. Wrap about 3"–4" of clothesline with fabric strip, overlapping fabric by about half the width of a strip (Photo B). Hold wraps in place with clothespin.

4. For an oval bowl, fold about 3" of wrapped clothesline back on itself. Begin stitching at center, catching beginning and adjacent coil (Photo C).

Turn fabric strips into a coiled bowl for a stylish home accessory.
Learn the basics, and then experiment to make assorted sizes and shapes.

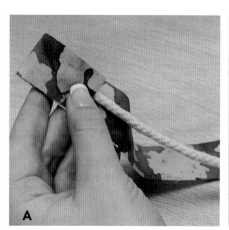

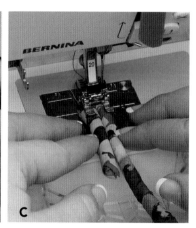

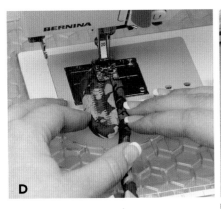

D

E

F

G

H

5. Coil clothesline clockwise, rotate bowl counterclockwise, and continue stitching *(Photo D)*.

6. To add a new fabric strip, begin about 1"–2" before end of previous strip. Wrap end of new strip tightly over end of previous strip; continue wrapping *(Photo E)*. Secure wraps with clothespin.

7. When bowl bottom is desired size, tip bowl bottom up and continue stitching to start forming sides of bowl *(Photo F)*.

8. Continue stitching around sides until bowl is desired size. Trim

end of clothesline, leaving about 4" of fabric strip *(Photo G)*. Twist fabric strip tightly over end of rope and beyond. Bring twisted fabric to inside of bowl and stitch down *(Photo H)*.

Sew Smart™

To form handles, simply loop wrapped clothesline to form handle. Stitch on handle area and then return to attaching wrapped clothesline to side of bowl.
—Joyce

Sew Smart™

For a round bowl, tightly coil wrapped clothesline clockwise. Rotate bowl counterclockwise as you continue around center *(Photo I)*. —Joyce

I

DESIGNER

As Creative Director for Sulky® of America, Joyce Drexler enjoys choosing colors and styles for new threads and designing projects that feature thread. Her book *Quick & Easy Weekend Quilting with Sulky®* is full of quick projects including more ideas for coiled fabric bowls. ❋

Love Note

Designer Mary Stori has been adding beads to her quilts and teaching beading techniques to students for years. Try your hand at embellishing a quilt with beads using Mary's techniques.

Size: 9½" × 9½"

MATERIALS

6" square white-on-white fabric for center background

5" square red solid for heart

¼ yard red-and-white print for borders and binding

5" square lightweight fusible web

Stabilizer for appliqué

White decorative thread to appliqué heart

About 50 (size 3) red bugle beads

About 1100 (size 11) white seed beads

Nymo (size D) white beading thread (or use white quilting thread)

Small embroidery hoop for beading

Chalk pencil or removable marking pen

11" square each backing fabric and batting

Cutting

Measurements include ¼" seam allowances.

From red-and-white print, cut:

• 1 (2½"-wide) strip. From strip, cut 2 (2½" × 6") top and bottom borders and 2 (2½" × 10") side borders.

• 2 (2¼"-wide) strips for binding.

Quilt Assembly

Heart pattern is on page 141. Follow manufacturer's instructions for using fusible web.

1. Trace heart onto paper side of fusible web; fuse web to wrong side of red square. Cut out heart on traced line.

2. Center heart on 6" white-on-white square; fuse in place. Use a decorative stitch to appliqué heart to background. (To prevent puckers, place stabilizer under the background fabric before stitching; remove when appliqué is complete.)

3. Add top and bottom borders to quilt.

4. Add side borders to quilt.

Embellishing

1. Trace the outline of heart and lettering on plain white paper and cut out. Use tape to secure paper atop appliquéd heart. With unthreaded sewing machine set at a short stitch, stitch atop the lettering to make reference marks on heart. Remove paper and trace letters, using removable marking pen or pencil.

2. Secure quilt top in small embroidery hoop. Bead the letters using white seed beads. (See *Sew Easy: Basic Beading* on page 142 for instructions.) Outline heart with red bugle beads.

Quilting and Finishing

1. Layer backing, batting, and quilt top; baste. Quilt as desired. Quilt shown was quilted in the ditch around the center square.

2. Join 2¼"-wide red-and-white binding strips into 1 continuous piece for straight-grain French-fold binding. Add binding to quilt.

3. Referring to *Sew Easy: Basic Beading* on page 142, add white seed beads to binding edge.

DESIGNER

Mary Stori is a nationally-known quilt designer, teacher, and author who loves to embellish her quilts and garments. She travels worldwide presenting lectures and workshops and escorting quilting tours. Look for Mary's book, *Beading Basics: 30 Embellishment Techniques for Quilters*, published by C & T Publishing. ✳

Pattern is shown full size. Add ³⁄₁₆" seam allowance for hand appliqué.

Sew Easy™ Basic Beading

Adding seed or bugle beads to a quilt can give it extra sparkle and character.
Try one or more of these techniques on your next project.

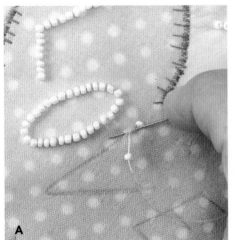

A

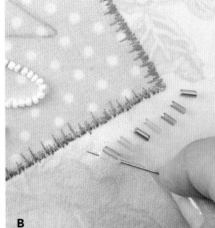

B

C

Mark design on fabric with removable pen or chalk pencil. For best results, secure work in a frame or hoop when beading. Stitch with a quilting between needle size 10 or 11 using Nymo size D beading thread or white quilting thread.

Beaded Lines or Lettering

1. Bring thread to top of work, coming up on marked line 1 bead width from beginning of line.

2. Place 1 seed bead on thread. Pass needle through the fabric at opposite side of bead (at beginning of line); bring needle back up through fabric on line, one bead width away from first bead. This attaches the bead with a back stitch.

3. Place next bead on thread and pass needle into fabric next to previous bead and back up on line, 1 bead width from previous bead (*Photo A*). Repeat as needed to bead all marked lines.

Attaching Bugle Beads

1. Bring thread to top of work at point where 1 end of bugle bead will be positioned.

2. Place 1 bugle bead on thread. Poke needle into fabric at end of bead, bringing needle underneath and back up at spot where next bugle bead will be (*Photo B*). Repeat to attach remaining bugle beads.

Beaded Binding

1. Bring needle out on fold of binding near 1 corner, hiding the knot under binding on wrong side of quilt. String 9 seed beads onto thread.

2. Pass needle through the binding edge at the end of 6th bead (*Photo C*). (Shortening the stitch causes the beads to form a slight arch.)

3. Bring needle back up at point you wish to start next arch. (On quilt shown, the arches are right next to each other, so needle comes up 1 bead width away.) Add beads and repeat stitching around binding.

Be Mine

Inspired by a visit to Winterset, Iowa, and the
romantic atmosphere surrounding the covered bridges of Madison County, Karina Hittle
designed these quilted valentines exclusively for *Love of Quilting* magazine.
Each valentine can be personalized for the one you love.

PROJECT RATING: INTERMEDIATE

Size: 5¾" × 8¾"

MATERIALS

NOTE: Fabrics in the projects shown are from Moda.

1 fat quarter★★ each of tan print and red stripe fabric for card and envelope

1 (5¾" × 8¾") rectangle heavyweight craft interfacing

1 (6"-long) piece each of (⅝"-wide) red ribbon and (½"-wide) lace

6 (⅝"-diameter) black flat suspender buttons

Typewriter key stickers

Printer-ready fabric for address labels

3" square each of dark red wool felt and light red wool felt for sealing wax embellishment on envelope

1 (⅝"-diameter) white hook and loop circle fastener

1 fat eighth★ red print for binding

1 each (1") and (½") heart button

Paper-backed fusible web

Freezer paper for templates

Fabric glue

★fat eighth = 9" × 20"

★★fat quarter = 18" × 20"

Cutting

Follow manufacturer's instructions for using fusible web. Patterns for appliqué pieces are on page 147.

From red stripe, cut:
- 1 (10½" × 17½") rectangle for envelope.
- 1 (5¾" × 8¾") rectangle for card.
- 1 Heart.

From tan print, cut:
- 1 (10½" × 17½") rectangle for envelope lining.
- 1 (5¾" × 8¾") rectangle for card.

From dark red wool felt, cut:
- 1 Wax piece.

From light red wool felt, cut:
- 1 Center piece.

From red print, cut:
- 2 (2¼"-wide) strips for binding.

Card Assembly

1. Using Placement Guide on heart pattern, mark line for top edge of lace on heart piece. Place top edge of lace on marked line and stitch in place.

2. Position bottom edge of ribbon slightly overlapping top edge of lace. Stitch in place along both edges of ribbon.

3. Cover front and back of interfacing rectangle with fusible web. Fuse tan print rectangle to front and red stripe rectangle to back of interfacing.

4. Quilt card as desired. Card shown is echo quilted in a rectangular shape.

5. Remove paper backing from heart. Fold ends of ribbon and lace to back of heart. Fuse heart to center of card front. Blanket stitch

around outside of heart above and below ribbon and lace trims.

6. Join 2¼"-wide red print strips into 1 continuous piece for straight-grain French-fold binding. Add binding to card.

7. Stitch black buttons in place, flat side up. Stick typewriter key letter stickers on top of buttons.

Envelope Assembly

1. Cover wrong side of red stripe envelope rectangle with fusible web. Fuse red stripe rectangle to tan print rectangle, wrong sides together. Trim fused rectangle to 9½" × 16¼".

2. Trace Envelope Flap Trim Line and Envelope Bottom Trim Line onto freezer paper. Iron freezer paper to envelope rectangle and cut on lines as shown in *Envelope Cutting Diagrams*.

3. Print or write address labels and fuse to front of envelope as shown in *Envelope Diagram*. Zigzag stitch around labels. Stitch large heart button to upper right corner on front of envelope.

4. Zigzag stitch along bottom of envelope to finish edge. Fold bottom of envelope to inside along lower fold line, aligning side edges; pin in place.

5. Beginning at bottom folded corner, zigzag stitch up the side; continue stitching up to point at top of envelope and down opposite side, ending at bottom folded corner.

6. Fuse light red Center to dark red Wax piece. Blanket stitch around Center. Stitch small heart button to center of sealing wax unit. Center unit on point of envelope, with part of unit extending over the edge. Straight stitch close to edge of sealing wax.

7. Glue loop side of fastener to point on inside of envelope. Fold top of envelope to back to determine placement for hook side of fastener; glue fastener in place on envelope back.

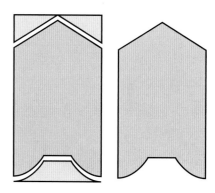

Envelope Cutting Diagrams

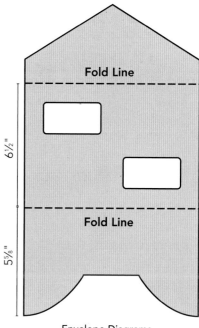

Envelope Diagrams

TRIED & TRUE

Karina made several versions of her quilted valentines in a variety of prints from Moda. She used a decorator tapestry fabric for one of the envelopes.

DESIGNER

Karina Hittle enjoys all forms of art. After more than twenty-five years of experience, she combined all of her artistic interests into the creation of her business Artful Offerings™. ✳

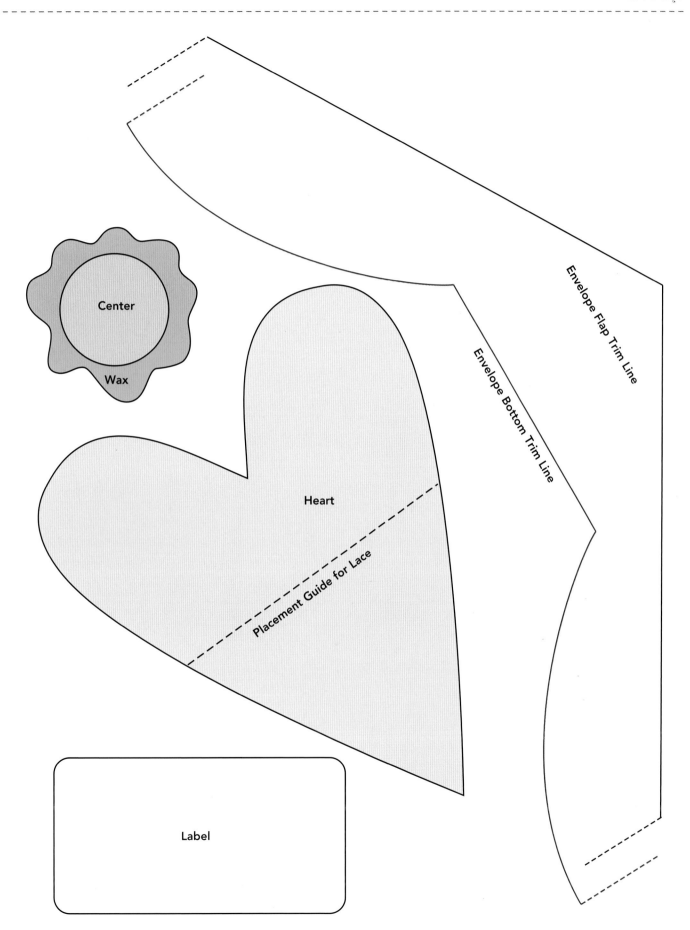

Center

Wax

Envelope Flap Trim Line

Envelope Bottom Trim Line

Heart

Placement Guide for Lace

Label

MADE BY **Madge Ziegler**.

Cathedral Window ORNAMENTS

The Cathedral Window is one of many Christmas ornament workshops Delaware quilter Madge Ziegler has taught at quilt shops in her area. Follow the steps to make this classic design for your tree. If you need a last minute gift, this could be it!

PROJECT RATING: EASY

Size: 4¼" × 4¼"

MATERIALS

(for one ornament)

2 (9") squares background fabric

2 (2½") squares window fabric

Polyester filler

Ribbon for hanging

Instructions

1. Fold (9") square in half right sides together. Using a ¼" seam, stitch across short ends (Photo A).

2. Open rectangle and line up seams. Stitch from center toward corners, leaving about 1¼" open in the center for turning (Photo B).

3. Turn, carefully pushing out corners. Press. Turn under seam allowance on opening and press flat (Photo C). Repeat Steps 1–3 for second unit.

4. Fold 4 corners in so points touch center and press to create creased guidelines (Photo D). Repeat for second unit.

5. Stitch 2 units together on opposite sides along crease lines to make a tube (Photo E).

6. Tack corners to centers (Photo F).

7. Roll tube so seams are at center on front and back. Center 1 (2½") square over seams that join units. Bring folded edges of background over raw edges of small square. Hand stitch using blind or other invisible appliqué stitch (Photo G). You may stitch through top only or all the way to the back.

8. Whip stitch bottom opening closed. Fill with polyester. Stitch top edges together, stuffing firmly before finishing top seam. Add ribbon bow tied with an extra loop for hanger.

Sew **Smart**™

Make a template with a 2½" square cut out of the center to take with you when shopping for novelty-type fabrics for your "windows." The template tells you if the motifs will fit in the window. —Liz ✳

DESIGNER

Madge Ziegler of Newark, Delaware, teaches and lectures throughout the Mid-Atlantic region. She is a past officer of the National Quilting Association. ✳

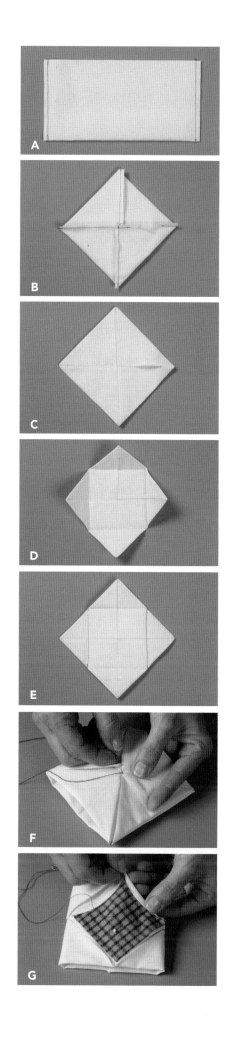

A

B

C

D

E

F

G

English Basket
ORNAMENT

The card stock pentagons used for English paper piecing this cute 3-D basket stay in permanently to help the basket retain its shape. Designer Madge Ziegler suggests you hang this ornament on your tree or fill it with tiny candies for a dinner favor.

PROJECT RATING: EASY
Size: approximately 1¼" tall, excluding handle

MATERIALS

(for one ornament)

3–4 index cards for paper-piecing templates

1 (2¼" × 20") strip each of 2 different Christmas prints, one for basket and one for lining

5 (7"-long) pieces ⅛"-wide wired metallic ribbon for handle (If you plan to hang the basket, you can use regular ribbon.)

Template plastic

Sewing thread to match fabrics

Spray temporary fabric adhesive

Seed beads to decorate top edge of basket (optional)

Cutting

Make template from pentagon pattern on page 151. To make a larger basket, enlarge pentagon pattern.

From index cards, cut:

• 12 pentagon pieces.

Sew Easy™

English Paper Piecing

Pentagon

Assembly

1. Refer to *Sew Easy: English Paper Piecing* to make basket.

2. Whipstitch around top edge of basket through 2 layers of fabric, catching end of 1 ribbon at top point of each pentagon. If desired, add beads to top edge of basket as you whipstitch around top edge.

3. Tie or twist ribbon ends together to form handle. If desired, add an additional bow at top of handle.

Sew **Smart**™

If you are using wire or wired ribbon, twist each piece 4 times around a fine dowel, skewer, or knitting needle to curl ribbon ends before joining them together. —Madge ✳

1. Fold 1 fabric strip in thirds. Lightly spray 2 paper templates with temporary adhesive and place atop folded fabric, leaving at least ½" between paper pieces to allow for seam allowances. Cut around paper pieces, adding ¼" seam allowance as you cut *(Photo A)*. You will have 6 matching pentagons. Repeat for second fabric.

2. Lightly spray wrong side of fabric pieces with temporary adhesive. Center 1 card stock pentagon atop each fabric piece *(Photo B)*.

Sew **Smart**™

Placing fabric pieces inside a cardboard box when spraying keeps the adhesive from accumulating on work surfaces. —Madge

---

3. Lightly spray card stock pentagons with temporary adhesive. Turn seam allowance over card stock around each piece *(Photo C)*.

4. Pair contrasting prepared pieces with paper sides facing. You will have 6 sets of paired pieces.

5. Hiding knots between pieces, whipstitch five paired pentagons to sides of basket bottom pair *(Photo D)*. You will be sewing through 4 fabric edges.

6. Join adjacent sides of pentagons to form basket *(Photo E)*. To pull the side edges together for stitching, you will need to slightly bend, not crease, each piece.

MADE BY **Julie Larsen**.

Holly Days
TABLE RUNNER

Stitch holly leaves and berries on a table runner to celebrate the joy of the season.

PROJECT RATING: EASY

Size: 15" × 32"

MATERIALS

½ yard black wool or felt

¼ yard green wool or felt

¼ yard red wool or felt

Green pearl cotton or embroidery
  floss

Gold and red embroidery floss

Freezer paper

Chalk pencil

Glue stick (optional)

Cutting

Make freezer paper templates from patterns on page 155. Press templates onto wool and cut out shapes from desired fabrics; remove paper.

From black wool, cut:

• 1 (15" × 32") rectangle.

From green wool, cut:

• 42 Leaves.

From red wool, cut:

• 256 Berries.

Table Runner Assembly

1. Using patterns on page 155, cut corner and side scallop templates from freezer paper. Referring to *Assembly Diagram*, draw scallops on black wool using chalk, evenly spacing scallops. Trim wool on marked line.

2. Arrange 3 Leaves and 8 pairs of Berries in each scallop as shown in *Assembly Diagram.*

NOTE: For dimension, berries are layered in pairs and attached to the background as one unit.

3. Using green pearl cotton or 2 strands of green embroidery floss, blanket stitch leaves to black background (*Blanket Stitch Diagram* on page 25).

4. Whipstitch layered berries in place, using 1 strand of red embroidery floss.

> ### Sew **Smart**™
> Tack Leaves and Berries in place with glue stick before stitching to background. —Marianne

5. Using 2 strands of gold embroidery floss, stitch stems and veins with a stem stitch (*Stem Stitch Diagram* on page 26).

6. Using 3 strands of red embroidery floss, blanket stitch around outer edge of table runner.

> ### Sew **Smart**™
> For step-by-step instructions on wool appliqué stitches, see *Sew Easy: Decorative Embroidery Stitches* on pages 25–27.

Assembly Diagram

SIZE OPTION: HOLLY DAYS TABLE TOPPER

We made a square version and added a vine.

Size: 16" × 16"

Cutting

1 (15") white square
1 (16") red square
48 red Berries
12 dark green Leaves
12 medium green Leaves
(⅜" x 37") medium green strip
  for vine

Assembly

Trim edges of white square as described in instructions on page 153. Referring to photo, stitch leaves, berries, and vine on white background. Stitch white piece on red square; trim red square ⅜" beyond edge of white piece. ✳

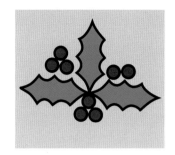

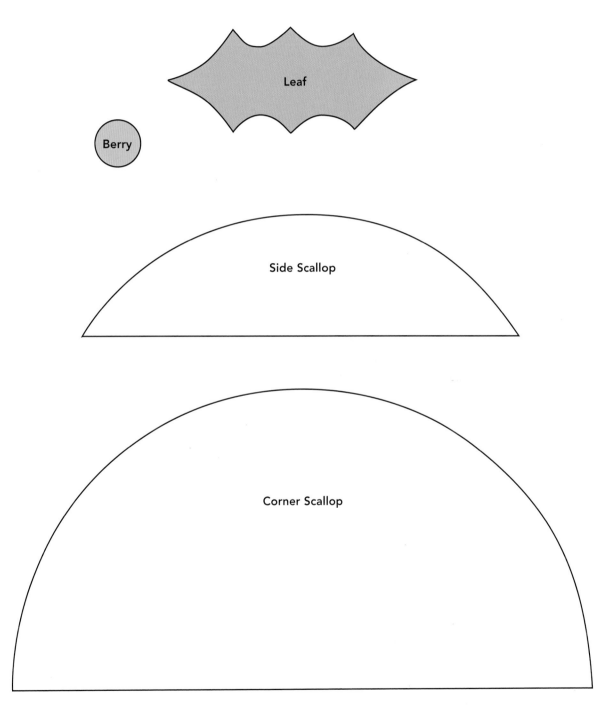

Leaf

Berry

Side Scallop

Corner Scallop

MADE BY **Madge Ziegler**.

Yo-Man & Yo-Landa

Designer Madge Ziegler varied traditional yo-yo construction methods to create a charming snow couple. Hang them on the tree or display them on a tabletop for the holiday season.

PROJECT RATING: EASY
Size: 3" tall

MATERIALS

NOTE: Small polka dots are great for hat fabrics because they look as though they are covered with tiny snowflakes. To give your snow couple a country look, use muslin or tan fabric for bodies instead of white.

⅛ yard white fabric for bodies

5" × 9" rectangle black print for Yo-man's hat

5" × 9" rectangle red print for Yo-landa's hat

10 orange seed beads for noses

21 black seed beads for eyes, mouths, and buttons

1 (5½"-long) piece of ⅛"-wide green satin ribbon

Black, red, and white quilting thread

1 yard white pearl cotton or crochet thread to assemble ornaments and for ornament hangers

Polyester fiberfill

3"-long tiny twig

Large darning or doll needle

Fine hand sewing needle that will fit through beads

Template material

Cutting for each couple

Make templates for circles from patterns on page 158.

From white fabric, cut:
- 4 Large Circles.
- 2 Small Circles.

From black print, cut:
- 1 Large Circle.
- 1 Small Circle.

From red print, cut:
- 1 Large Circle.
- 1 Small Circle.

Assembly

1. Tie a large knot at 1 end of length of white quilting thread. (We used black thread to be more visible in photos.) To make 1 stuffed body circle, sew ¼"-long running stitches ³⁄₁₆" from edge of 1 large white circle. Draw up thread slightly; insert polyester fiberfill to fill circle (*Photo A*). Draw thread tight around stuffed circle and knot thread. Repeat for remaining white circles. In a similar manner, use large black

circle and black thread to create stuffed circle for Yo-man's hat.

> ### Sew **Smart**™
> The amount of stuffing you use will affect the appearance of your snow people. Each will look different, but you will want to stuff fairly firmly. —Madge

2. For Yo-landa's beret, make a traditional yo-yo from small red circle. Fold under ¼" around perimeter of circle as you run a basting stitch with red thread around the circle. Pull up stitching to gather yo-yo; knot thread (*Photo B*). Repeat to make a traditional yo-yo from the large red circle for Yo-landa's beret and from the small black circle for Yo-man's hat brim.

3. To assemble Yo-landa, thread darning or doll needle with 18"-long piece of pearl cotton or crochet thread. Leaving a 4"–5" thread tail when you begin, string

pieces together by going through yo-yos in the following order: gathered side of small red yo-yo, gathered side of large red yo-yo, smooth end of small white stuffed circle, knotted ends of 2 large white stuffed circles. Reinsert needle about ⅛" from where you came out and go back up through all 5 pieces (*Photo C*). Pull up thread firmly and knot; knot again about 3" away from first knot to create hanger. Trim ends of thread.

4. In a similar manner, string Yo-man together in the following order: smooth end of stuffed black yo-yo, gathered side of traditional black yo-yo, smooth end of small white stuffed circle, knotted ends of 2 large white stuffed circles.

5. Use a pencil to lightly mark position for eyes, nose, mouth, and buttons on each snow person.

6. Thread beading needle with black quilting thread and tie knot at 1 end. Begin stitching under

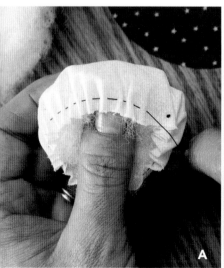

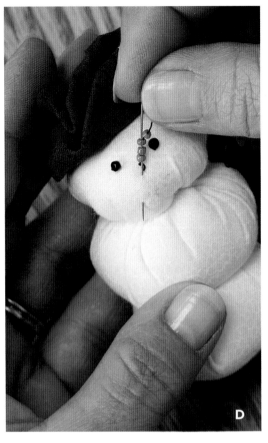

Yo-landa's hat so knot will be hidden. Bring needle out at spot for 1 eye and stitch on 1 black bead; come up at spot for second eye and add bead. Next, come up at spot for nose, string 4 orange beads onto thread, insert thread in second bead from end and go back through remaining beads, insert back into nose position *(Photo D)*. Nose will stand out from face. Come up at 1 end of mouth spot, sew on 3 or 4 black beads for mouth. Come

up at spots for buttons and add 1 black bead for each button; knot thread and pop knot into body. Tie green ribbon around neck. Using the same method, add bead facial features to Yo-man, but use 5–6 orange beads for nose and 5–6 black beads for mouth. Add buttons; come out at side of bottom circle and stitch twig in place. Knot thread and pop knot into body. Stitch top of twig to Yo-man's hat brim. ✻

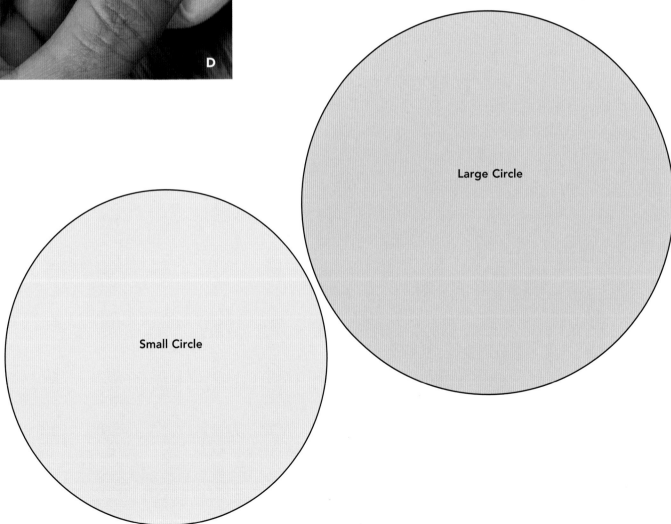

Large Circle

Small Circle

BY **Members of the Piece of Work quilt group; Joni Reed Cooley, Sharon Nosek, Sandy Pape, Liz Varnum, and Kim Whiting.**

50 Secret Sister Gifts

1. Give a fragrant votive candle.
2. Stitch a redwork penny square.
3. Decorate a notebook cover (see page 117).
4. Make a guild nametag.
5. Cut a few fat quarters.
6. Make a quilted pen.
7. Cut a stack of scrap squares.
8. Make a pincushion (see pages 20 & 28).
9. Make some quilt labels.
10. Make a small notions bag (see page 31).
11. Make a potholder.
12. Make a needlecase (see pages 23 & 34).
13. "Recycle" a gently-used book.
14. Share some favorite recipes.
15. Take a roll of photos at your next retreat to give to her.
16. Select some cute buttons and decorate a button box (see page 37).
17. Chocolate.
18. Make a padded, vibration-reducing mat for under her sewing machine (see page 159).
19. Pick out some seed packets.
20. Make a small paper-pieced gift basket.
21. Make a booklet of your favorite quilt-related sayings.
22. Bake some homemade goodies.
23. Give a 1" × 6" ruler.
24. Make a purse with matching billfold, coin purse, and tissue holder (see page 98).
25. Select yummy coffee or tea packets.
26. Find a quilty magnet or necklace.
27. Find some copyright-free patterns and put them together in a notebook.
28. Frame a block.
29. Give a spool of variegated thread.
30. Create a quilt block pattern named just for her.
31. Give a needle assortment.
32. Make a set of hanging ruler holders (see page 16).
33. Put together a small needle punch project (see page 132).
34. Send her a list of your favorite quilting tips.
35. Make a keychain.
36. Make a bookmark.
37. Select a chalk marking pencil.
38. Make a thread cutter necklace.
39. Make an easy table runner (see pages 134 & 152).
40. Make a fun pillowcase from novelty fabrics (see page 123).
41. Make a set of placemats.
42. Make some pretty coasters.
43. Give a favorite lip balm.
44. Make a seat cushion.
45. Give a disposable camera for fun retreat photos.
46. "Recycle" a handy quilting notion that you have not used.
47. Give a purse-size, oil free hand lotion.
48. Make a friendship signature quilt (see page 127).
49. Give a project kit.
50. Surrender a whole yard of fabric.

Happy Holidays

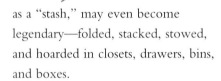

BY **Linda Hungerford**.

Shopping
for Your Favorite Quilter

If your loved ones are unenlightened about quilting but want to give gifts that make you smile, place this article strategically so they can learn the rudiments of your passion.

Quilt shop staff members can be just the Santa's helpers you need to choose a gorgeous group of fabrics. Be sure to buy at least three yards of each!

More Fabric?

"Isn't this new Moda™ print luscious? It works perfectly with those new marbles I got last week," she says.

He glances blankly at the fabric bolt and her glowing face. "She has piles of it already," he thinks, "so why does she need more?"

This is the question that plagues the mind of a man whose wife is obsessed with quilting.

Enlighten Yourself

Quilters are visually attracted to the colors and textures of fabric and so they steadily accumulate it. A fabric collection, known among quilters as a "stash," may even become legendary—folded, stacked, stowed, and hoarded in closets, drawers, bins, and boxes.

Non-quilting husbands, mothers, sisters, children, and friends may wonder, "What's her attraction to fabric? Why so many quilting supplies?"

The answer is that fabric and related supplies are essential for successful quilt making. Also, it's just plain fun to own the newest fabric, the latest book, and the most innovative quilting notions.

Once you have a basic understanding of the process, you'll be able to shop for and confidently select holiday and birthday gifts with your favorite quilter in mind.

Fabric Shopping
Basics

When fabric shopping, remember two important things. Fabrics must be 100 percent cotton (no polyester, please) and in the colors your favorite quilter loves. You'll find cottons for quilting in a quilt shop or fabric store.

Fabric comes in a myriad of colors and designs from dozens of manufacturers. The selection may

Photographed on location by Craig Anderson. Many thanks to Vince, V.J., Devin, and Alex Mandi, and to Mark Davis and Cindy Bortell for participating in our photos.

A subscription to your favorite quilter's favorite quilting magazine (*Love of Quilting*, perhaps?) can make the perfect stocking stuffer.

seem endless (it almost is!), but don't be daunted by the choices. Select a printed design or solid color that is:

- your favorite quilter's preferred color
- your favorite quilter's preferred style–flowers, geometric designs, small prints, novelty prints, designer lines, period reproductions, etc.
- white, ivory or any neutral color (for backgrounds).

Fat Quarters

Buy fat quarters. A fat quarter is a fourth yard of fabric cut in very usable dimensions (18" × 20"). If fat quarters aren't available, ask for a regular fourth yard (9" × 40").

Twenty Gifts to Give the Quilter You Love

1. **Fabric, "material," "fat quarters"**—the cotton stuff of which quilts are made.
2. **A basic, how-to-quilt reference book.**
3. **A newly released quilting book** recommended by your local quilt shop.
4. **Quilter's rulers** of various shapes and dimensions.
5. **Rotary cutter** in a new size or style.
6. **Replacement rotary cutter blades.**
7. **Hand or machine sewing needles.**
8. **Thread.** Choose cotton thread in neutral, gray, white, your quilter's favorite colors, or a gift-boxed color assortment.
9. **Scissors.** Whether they're small, fold-up, snips, appliqué, or dressmaker-sized, select good quality, durable scissors.
10. **Paper and plastic.** Tracing paper, freezer paper, foundation paper, and template plastic make quilt making easier.
11. **Marking tools.** Select fabric pencils and pens, washable markers, and white and colored fabric chalk.
12. **Storage containers.** Choose clear plastic containers and bags so the contents can be seen at a glance.
13. **Quilting calendar.** Wall- or desk-sized, choose one with quilting tips or with instructions for making the featured quilts or blocks.
14. **Lamp or light bulb.** Select models designed to help a quilter see more clearly.
15. **Quilting software.** If your favorite quilter is comfortable at a computer, choose software that allows her to design quilts or print quilt blocks.
16. **Gift certificate.** Let your favorite quilter choose fabrics, books, notions, or to have a quilt top professionally machine quilted.
17. **Membership dues.** Give the gift of continuing education through membership in a quilt guild or another quilting organization.
18. **Magazine subscription.** Extend her current subscription or give her a new treat in her mailbox.
19. **Sewing machine.** A reliable sewing machine is a quilt making necessity. A sewing machine is a gift that continues to give, so be sure to buy the highest quality and value you can afford. Ask her advice on this one.
20. **Time.** Quilters can't get enough of it. Give your favorite quilter a homemade coupon booklet redeemable for tasks that free her for quilt play.

Fabrics and books are easier to select if you know the colors and the types of projects your quilter likes to use and make.

Book Shopping

Books about quilting are essential. They're instructional, inspirational, and contain directions to make particular projects. Categories are:

❦ "How-to" or reference books. Select one that includes quilting basics–everything from fabric selection, machine piecing, and appliqué techniques, to layering, quilting, and binding.

❦ Basic block books. These books are great for identifying the pattern of an antique quilt purchased at a garage sale or inherited from a family member.

❦ Educational books. Expand quilt making options with books emphasizing a particular style or technique–samplers, row-by-row, appliqué, redwork, borders, color, or machine and hand quilting.

❦ Fun and relaxation titles. If she enjoys reading, give her a fiction title that has quilt making as an integral part of the story. Audio books are terrific. She can listen while she stitches. Ask for the most popular titles at a bookstore or online bookstore.

Notions Shopping

Notions, gadgets, and tools are simply the paraphernalia available to make quilt making easier. Some notions are designed specifically for quilters, and other gadgets are mainstream products for which quilters find new uses. The categories are:

❦ Measuring and cutting. Rulers, rotary cutters, and rotary cutting mats are much-used tools that speed up cutting. Your quilter may already have the necessities, but one is never enough. Just be sure to select rulers designed especially for quilt making. They're made from clear acrylic with black or colored markings. Rotary cutters and rotary cutting mats come in assorted sizes, too. (To avoid damaging work surfaces, a rotary cutter must be used in tandem with a rotary cutting mat.)

❦ Stitching and sewing. A quilter may have a thread preference, but, in general, most use cotton thread for piecing, cotton or a cotton/silk blend for appliqué, and cotton, cotton/silk, and rayon

threads for machine quilting. "Quilting thread" is strictly for hand quilting. Frequently used colors are gray, taupe, or off-white for piecing and white or neutral for quilting. For appliqué work, select thread in a color that matches the fabric.

❦ Marking and pinning. To complete a quilt, your favorite quilter may either hire a professional hand- or machine-quilter (a gift certificate opportunity for you!) or, she will quilt it herself. If she's quilting it herself, she may need to mark the quilt top with quilting designs.

Shop for books of quilt designs, plastic pre-cut templates, or uncut sheets of plastic so she can create her own quilt designs. She may need tracing paper, a chalk-filled pouncing pad, a special quilter's pencil, or a chalk pencil to transfer a quilting design to the quilt top. Quilt shop staff can help you choose.

After marking, the quilt is sandwiched, using batting between the top and bottom layers of fabric. Cotton, polyester, and wool batts come in twin, queen and king sizes, and by the yard. Check with your favorite quilter to determine her

No matter how much you spend, remember that it's cheaper and more politically correct than a new mink.

Five Questions to Ask Your Favorite Quilter Before Shopping

For better insight into your favorite quilter's personal preferences, and to discover worthwhile gift-giving ideas, get her answers to these questions:

1. What colors are in your favorite color palette?

2. What is your favorite quilt design or style?

3. What brand of sewing machine do you sew with?

4. How do you prefer to finish your quilts?

5. Which quilting magazines are your favorites?

preference, or consider giving her a gift certificate.

The quilt sandwich may be basted with a needle and thread, safety pins, plastic tacks "shot" from a gun, or with basting spray. Try shopping for basting notions that help expand her experience.

❧ Getting it together. An array of storage options is available to help your favorite quilter get organized. Consider these items: a rack to hold quilting rulers in an upright position, a magnetic bobbin case, transparent plastic zipper bags, three-hole plastic holders to put magazines in, and large canvas bags. Shop for containers and carts at mainline stores. Clear plastic boxes hold thread and fabric and help organize separate projects. Wheeled, plastic drawer sets or mechanic's tool chests permit a quilter to roll supplies to a sewing machine or a quilting retreat.

Give Her Time

If fabrics, books, or notions aren't in your budget, the most priceless gift can be the gift of time. Give her coupons from you or the kids for one-hour increments of uninterrupted sewing time. Coupons may designate time spent watching children, fixing and serving meals, grocery shopping, or taking on other time-relieving tasks.

Whatever gift you select, you'll make your favorite quilter a happier quilter, and you'll be rewarded with a grateful smile, and maybe even a quilt to wrap up in! ✳

| QUILTER'S COUPON | NO EXPIRATION DATE |

FREE Quilting Hour

When you need an uninterrupted hour for your quilting project.

You may redeem this coupon anytime.

General Instructions

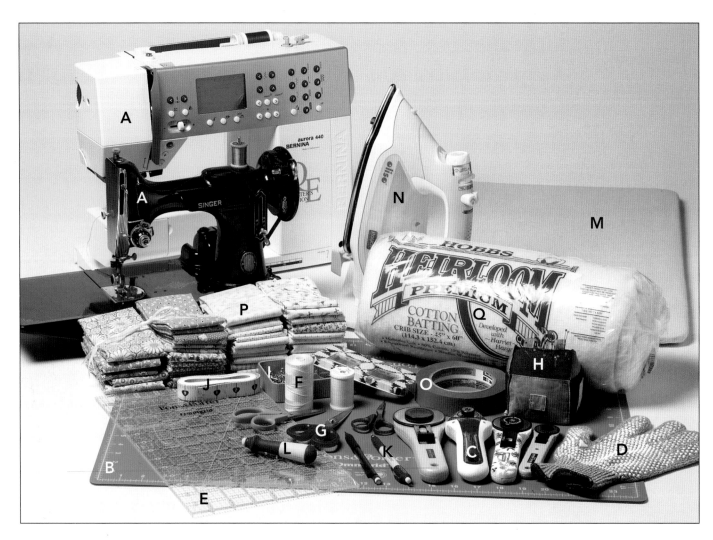

Basic Supplies

You'll need a **sewing machine (A)** in good working order to construct patchwork blocks, join blocks together, add borders, and machine quilt. We encourage you to purchase a machine from a local dealer, who can help you with service in the future, rather than from a discount store. Another option may be to borrow a machine from a friend or family member. If the machine has not been used in a while, have it serviced by a local dealer to make sure it is in good working order. If you need an extension cord, one with a surge protector is a good idea.

A **rotary cutting mat (B)** is essential for accurate and safe rotary cutting. Purchase one that is no smaller than 18" × 24".

Rotary cutting mats are made of "self-healing" material that can be used over and over.

A **rotary cutter (C)** is a cutting tool that looks like a pizza cutter, and has a very sharp blade. We recommend starting with a standard size 45mm rotary cutter. Always lock or close your cutter when it is not in use, and keep it out of the reach of children.

A **safety glove** (also known as a *Klutz Glove)* **(D)** is also recommended. Wear your safety glove on the hand that is holding the ruler in place. Because it is made of cut-resistant material, the safety glove protects your non-cutting hand from accidents that can occur if your cutting hand slips while cutting.

An acrylic **ruler (E)** is used in combination with your cutting mat and rotary cutter. We recommend the Fons & Porter

8" × 14" ruler, but a 6" × 12" ruler is another good option. You'll need a ruler with inch, quarter-inch, and eighth-inch markings that show clearly for ease of measuring. Choose a ruler with 45-degree-angle, 30-degree-angle, and 60-degree-angle lines marked on it as well.

Since you will be using 100% cotton fabric for your quilts, use **cotton or cotton-covered polyester thread (F)** for piecing and quilting. Avoid 100% polyester thread, as it tends to snarl.

Keep a pair of small **scissors (G)** near your sewing machine for cutting threads.

Thin, good quality **straight pins (H)** are preferred by quilters. The pins included with pin cushions are normally too thick to use for piecing, so discard them. Purchase a box of nickel-plated brass **safety pins** size #1 **(I)** to use for pin-basting the layers of your quilt together for machine quilting.

Invest in a 120"-long dressmaker's **measuring tape (J)**. This will come in handy when making borders for your quilt.

A 0.7–0.9mm mechanical **pencil (K)** works well for marking on your fabric.

Invest in a quality sharp **seam ripper (L)**. Every quilter gets well-acquainted with her seam ripper!

Set up an **ironing board (M)** and **iron (N)** in your sewing area. Pressing yardage before cutting, and pressing patchwork seams as you go are both essential for quality quiltmaking. Select an iron that has steam capability.

Masking **tape (O)** or painter's tape works well to mark your sewing machine so you can sew an accurate ¼" seam. You will also use tape to hold your backing fabric taut as you prepare your quilt sandwich for machine quilting.

The most exciting item that you will need for quilting is **fabric (P)**. Quilters generally prefer 100% cotton fabrics for their quilts. This fabric is woven from cotton threads, and has a lengthwise and a crosswise grain. The term "bias" is used to describe the diagonal grain of the fabric. If you make a 45-degree angle cut through a square of cotton fabric, the cut edges will be bias edges, which are quite stretchy. As you learn more quiltmaking techniques, you'll learn how bias can work to your advantage or disadvantage.

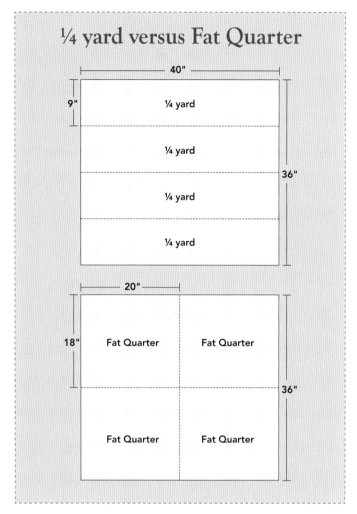

¼ yard versus Fat Quarter

Fabric is sold by the yard at quilt shops and fabric stores. Quilting fabric is generally about 40"–44" wide, so a yard is about 40" wide by 36" long. As you collect fabrics to build your own personal stash, you will buy yards, half yards (about 18" × 40"), quarter yards (about 9" × 40"), as well as other lengths.

Many quilt shops sell "fat quarters," a special cut favored by quilters. A fat quarter is created by cutting a half yard down the fold line into two 18" × 20" pieces (fat quarters) that are sold separately. Quilters like the nearly square shape of the fat quarter because it is more useful than the narrow regular quarter yard cut.

Batting (Q) is the filler between quilt top and backing that makes your quilt a quilt. It can be cotton, polyester, cotton-polyester blend, wool, silk, or other natural materials, such as bamboo or corn. Make sure the batting you buy is at least six inches wider and six inches longer than your quilt top.

Accurate Cutting

Measuring and cutting accuracy are important for successful quilting. Measure at least twice, and cut once!

Cut strips across the fabric width unless directed otherwise.

Cutting for patchwork usually begins with cutting strips, which are then cut into smaller pieces. First, cut straight strips from a fat quarter:

1. Fold fat quarter in half with selvage edge at the top (*Photo A*).

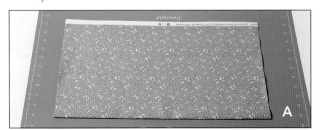

2. Straighten edge of fabric by placing ruler atop fabric, aligning one of the lines on ruler with selvage edge of fabric (*Photo B*). Cut along right edge of ruler.

3. Rotate fabric, and use ruler to measure from cut edge to desired strip width (*Photo C*). Measurements in instructions include ¼" seam allowances.

4. After cutting the required number of strips, cut strips into squares and label them.

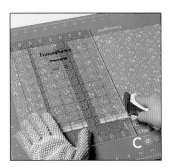

Setting up Your Sewing Machine

Sew Accurate ¼" Seams

Standard seam width for patchwork and quiltmaking is ¼". Some machines come with a patchwork presser foot, also known as a quarter-inch foot. If your machine doesn't have a quarter-inch foot, you may be able to purchase one from a dealer. Or, you can create a quarter-inch seam guide on your machine using masking tape or painter's tape.

Place an acrylic ruler on your sewing machine bed under the presser foot. Slowly turn handwheel until the tip of the needle barely rests atop the ruler's quarter-inch mark (*Photo A*). Make sure the lines on the ruler are parallel to the lines on the machine throat plate. Place tape on the machine bed along edge of ruler (*Photo B*).

Take a Simple Seam Test

Seam accuracy is critical to machine piecing, so take this simple test once you have your quarter-inch presser foot on your machine or have created a tape guide.

Place 2 (2½") squares right sides together, and sew with a scant ¼" seam. Open squares and finger press seam. To finger press, with right sides facing you, press the seam to one side with your fingernail. Measure across pieces, raw edge to raw edge (*Photo C*). If they measure 4½", you have passed the test! Repeat the test as needed to make sure you can confidently sew a perfect ¼" seam.

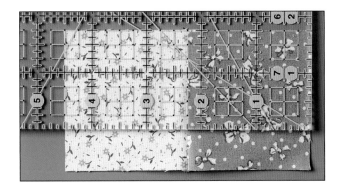

Sewing Comfortably

Other elements that promote pleasant sewing are good lighting, a comfortable chair, background music—and chocolate! Good lighting promotes accurate sewing. The better you can see what you are working on, the better your results. A comfortable chair enables you to sew for longer periods of time. An office chair with a good back rest and adjustable height works well. Music helps keep you relaxed. Chocolate is, for many quilters, simply a necessity.

Tips for Patchwork and Pressing

As you sew more patchwork, you'll develop your own shortcuts and favorite methods. Here are a few favored by many quilters:

● As you join patchwork units to form rows, and join rows to form blocks, press seams in opposite directions from row to row whenever possible (*Photo A*). By pressing seams one direction in the first row and the opposite direction in the next row, you will often create seam allowances that abut when rows are joined (*Photo B*). Abutting or nesting seams are ideal for forming perfectly matched corners on the right side of your quilt blocks and quilt top. Such pressing is not always possible, so don't worry if you end up with seam allowances facing the same direction as you join units.

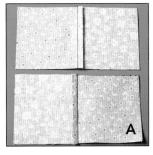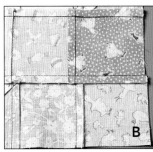

● Sew on and off a small, folded fabric square to prevent bobbin thread from bunching at throat plate (*Photo C*). You'll also save thread, which means fewer stops to wind bobbins, and fewer hanging threads to be snipped. Repeated use of the small piece of fabric gives it lots of thread "legs," so some quilters call it a spider.

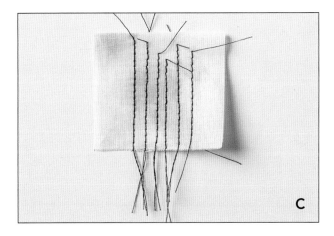

- Chain piece patchwork to reduce the amount of thread you use, and minimize the number and length of threads you need to trim from patchwork. Without cutting threads at the end of a seam, take 3–4 stitches without any fabric under the needle, creating a short thread chain approximately ⅛" long (*Photo D*). Repeat until you have a long line of pieces. Remove chain from machine, clip threads between units, and press seams.

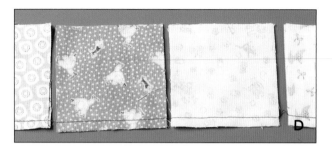

- Trim off tiny triangle tips (sometimes called dog ears) created when making triangle-square units (*Photo E*). Trimming triangles reduces bulk and makes patchwork units and blocks lie flatter. Though no one will see the back of your quilt top once it's quilted, a neat back free of dangling threads and patchwork points is the mark of a good quilter. Also, a smooth, flat quilt top is easier to quilt, whether by hand or machine.

- Careful pressing will make your patchwork neat and crisp, and will help make your finished quilt top lie flat. Ironing and pressing are two different skills. Iron fabric to remove wrinkles using a back and forth, smoothing motion. Press patchwork and quilt blocks by raising and gently lowering the iron atop your work. After sewing a patchwork unit, first press the seam with the unit closed, pressing to set, or embed, the stitching. Setting the seam this way will help produce straight, crisp seams. Open the unit and press on the right side with the seam toward the darkest fabric, being careful to not form a pleat in your seam, and carefully pressing the patchwork flat.

- Many quilters use finger pressing to open and flatten seams of small units before pressing with an iron. To finger press, open patchwork unit with right side of fabric facing you. Run your fingernail firmly along seam, making sure unit is fully open with no pleat.

- Careful use of steam in your iron will make seams and blocks crisp and flat (*Photo F*). Aggressive ironing can stretch blocks out of shape, and is a common pitfall for new quilters.

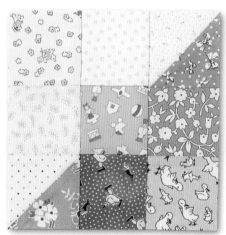

Adding Borders

Follow these simple instructions to make borders that fit perfectly on your quilt.

1. Find the length of your quilt by measuring through the quilt center, not along the edges, since the edges may have stretched. Take 3 measurements and average them to determine the length to cut your side borders (*Diagram A*). Cut 2 side borders this length.

2. Fold border strips in half to find center. Pinch to create crease mark or place a pin at center. Fold quilt top in half crosswise to find center of side. Attach side borders to quilt center by pinning them at the ends and the center, and easing in any fullness. If quilt edge is a bit longer than border, pin and sew with border on top; if border is

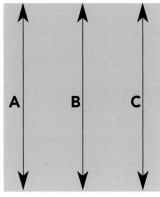

Diagram A

A _____

B _____

C _____

TOTAL _____

÷3
_____

AVERAGE
LENGTH _____

HELPFUL TIP
Use the following decimal conversions to calculate
your quilt's measurements:

⅛" = .125	⅝" = .625
¼" = .25	¾" = .75
⅜" = .375	⅞" = .875
½" = .5	

slightly longer than quilt top, pin and sew with border on the bottom. Machine feed dogs will ease in the fullness of the longer piece. Press seams toward borders.

3. Find the width of your quilt by measuring across the quilt and side borders (*Diagram B*). Take 3 measurements and average them to determine the length to cut your top and bottom borders. Cut 2 borders this length.

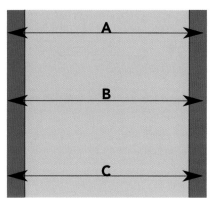

Diagram B

4. Mark centers of borders and top and bottom edges of quilt top. Attach top and bottom borders to quilt, pinnning at ends and center, and easing in any fullness (*Diagram C*). Press seams toward borders.

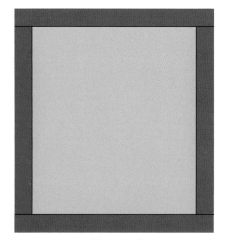

Diagram C

5. Gently steam press entire quilt top on one side and then the other. When pressing on wrong side, trim off any loose threads.

Joining Border Strips

Not all quilts have borders, but they are a nice complement to a quilt top. If your border is longer than 40", you will need to join 2 or more strips to make a border the required length. You can join border strips with either a straight seam parallel to the ends of the strips (*Photo A on page 170*), or with a diagonal seam. For the diagonal seam method, place one border strip perpendicular to another strip, rights sides facing (*Photo B*). Stitch diagonally across strips as shown. Trim seam allowance to ¼". Press seam open (*Photo C*).

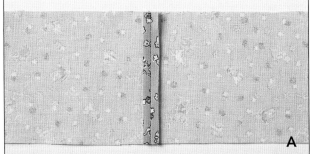

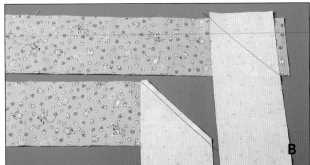

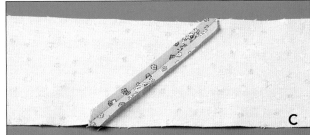

Quilting Your Quilt

Quilters today joke that there are three ways to quilt a quilt—by hand, by machine, or by check. Some enjoy making quilt tops so much, they prefer to hire a professional machine quilter to finish their work. The Split Nine Patch baby quilt shown at left has simple machine quilting that you can do yourself.

Decide what color thread will look best on your quilt top before choosing your backing fabric. A thread color that will blend in with the quilt top is a good choice for beginners. Choose backing fabric that will blend with your thread as well. A print fabric is a good choice for hiding less-than-perfect machine quilting. The backing fabric must be at least 3"–4" larger than your quilt top on all 4 sides. For example: if your quilt top measures 44" × 44", your backing needs to be at least 50" × 50". If your quilt top is 80" × 96", then your backing fabric needs to be at least 86" × 102".

For quilt tops 36" wide or less, use a single width of fabric for the backing. Buy enough length to allow adequate margin at quilt edges, as noted above. When your quilt is wider than 36", one option is to use 60"-, 90"-, or 108"-wide fabric for the quilt backing. Because fabric selection is limited for wide fabrics, quilters generally piece the quilt backing from 44/45"-wide fabric. Plan on 40"–42" of usable fabric width when estimating how much fabric to purchase. Plan your piecing strategy to avoid having a seam along the vertical or horizontal center of the quilt.

For a quilt 37"–60" wide, a backing with horizontal seams is usually the most economical use of fabric. For example, for a quilt 50" × 70", vertical seams would require 152", or 4¼ yards, of 44/45"-wide fabric (76" + 76" = 152"). Horizontal seams would require 112", or 3¼ yards (56" + 56" = 112").

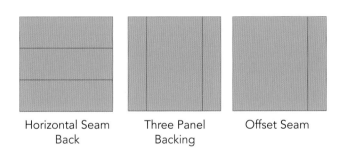

Horizontal Seam Back   Three Panel Backing   Offset Seam

For a quilt 61"–80" wide, most quilters piece a three-panel backing, with vertical seams, from two lengths of fabric. Cut one of the pieces in half lengthwise, and sew the halves to opposite sides of the wider panel. Press the seams away from the center panel.

For a quilt 81"–120" wide, you will need three lengths of fabric, plus extra margin. For example, for a quilt 108" × 108", purchase at least 342", or 9½ yards, of 44/45"-wide fabric (114" + 114" + 114" = 342").

For a three-panel backing, pin the selvage edge of the center panel to the selvage edge of the side panel, with edges aligned and right sides facing. Machine stitch with a ½" seam. Trim seam allowances to ¼", trimming off the selvages from both panels at once. Press the seam away from the center of the quilt. Repeat on other side of center panel.

For a two-panel backing, join panels in the same manner as above, and press the seam to one side.

Create a "quilt sandwich" by layering your backing, batting, and quilt top. Find the crosswise center of the backing fabric by folding it in half. Mark with a pin on each side. Lay backing down on a table or floor, wrong side up. Tape corners and edges of backing to the surface with masking or painter's tape so that backing is taut (*Photo A*).

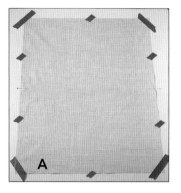

Fold batting in half crosswise and position it atop backing fabric, centering folded edge at center of backing (*Photo B*). Unfold batting and smooth it out atop backing (*Photo C*).

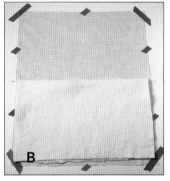
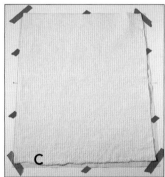

In the same manner, fold the quilt top in half crosswise and center it atop backing and batting (*Photo D*). Unfold top and smooth it out atop batting (*Photo E*).

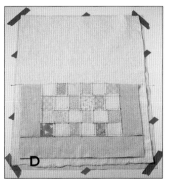

Use safety pins to pin baste the layers (*Photo F*). Pins should be about a fist width apart. A special tool, called a Kwik Klip, or a grapefruit spoon makes closing the pins easier. As you slide a pin through all three layers, slide the point of the pin into one of the tool's grooves. Push on the tool to help close the pin.

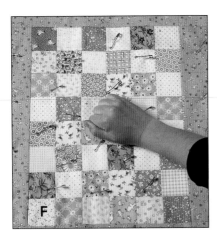

For straight line quilting, install an even feed or walking foot on your machine. This presser foot helps all three layers of your quilt move through the machine evenly without bunching.

Walking Foot   Stitching "in the ditch"

An easy way to quilt your first quilt is to stitch "in the ditch" along seam lines. No marking is needed for this type of quilting.

Binding Your Quilt

Preparing Binding

Strips for quilt binding may be cut either on the straight of grain or on the bias. For the quilts in this booklet, cut strips on the straight of grain.

1. Measure the perimeter of your quilt and add approximately 24" to allow for mitered corners and finished ends.

2. Cut the number of strips necessary to achieve desired length. We like to cut binding strips 2¼" wide.

3. Join your strips with diagonal seams into 1 continuous piece (*Photo A*). Press the seams open. (See page 169 for instructions for the diagonal seams method of joining strips.)

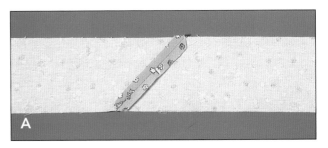

4. Press your binding in half lengthwise, with wrong sides facing, to make French-fold binding (*Photo B*).

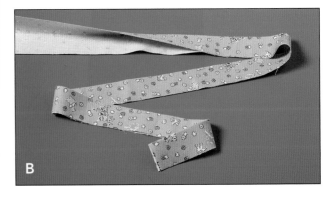

Attaching Binding

Attach the binding to your quilt using an even-feed or walking foot. This prevents puckering when sewing through the three layers.

1. Choose beginning point along one side of quilt. Do not start at a corner. Match the two raw edges of the binding strip to the raw edge of the quilt top. The folded edge

will be free and to left of seam line (*Photo C*). Leave 12" or longer tail of binding strip dangling free from beginning point. Stitch, using ¼" seam, through all layers.

2. For mitered corners, stop stitching ¼" from corner; backstitch, and remove quilt from sewing machine (*Photo D*). Place a pin ¼" from corner to mark where you will stop stitching.

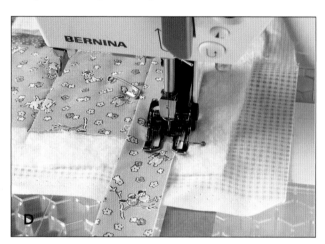

Rotate quilt quarter turn and fold binding straight up, away from corner, forming 45-degree-angle fold (*Photo E*).

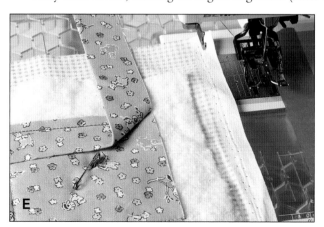

Bring binding straight down in line with next edge to be sewn, leaving top fold even with raw edge of previously sewn side (*Photo F*). Begin stitching at top edge, sewing through all layers (*Photo G*).

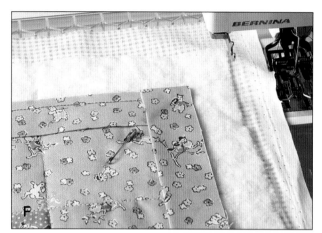

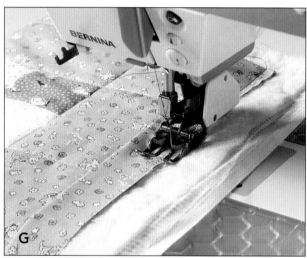

3. To finish binding, stop stitching about 8" away from starting point, leaving about a 12" tail at end (*Photo H*). Bring beginning and end of binding to center of 8" opening and fold each back, leaving about ¼" space

between the two folds of binding (*Photo I*). (Allowing this ¼" extra space is critical, as binding tends to stretch when it is stitched to the quilt. If the folded ends meet at this point, your binding will be too long for the space after the ends are joined.) Crease folds of binding with your fingernail.

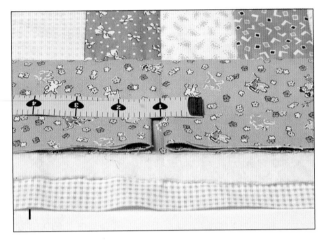

4. Open out each edge of binding and draw line across wrong side of binding on creased fold line, as shown in *Photo J*. Draw line along lengthwise fold of binding at same spot to create an X (*Photo K*).

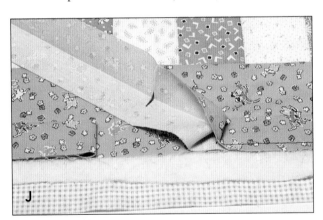

5. With edge of ruler at marked X, line up 45-degree-angle marking on ruler with one long side of binding (*Photo L*). Draw diagonal line across binding as shown in *Photo M*.

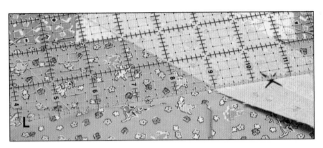

Repeat for other end of binding. Lines must angle in same direction (*Photo N*).

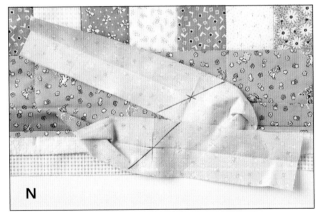

6. Pin binding ends together with right sides facing, pin-matching diagonal lines as shown in *Photo O*. Binding ends will be at right angles to each other. Machine-stitch along diagonal line, removing pins as you stitch (*Photo P*).

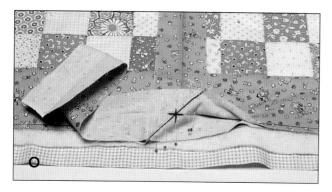

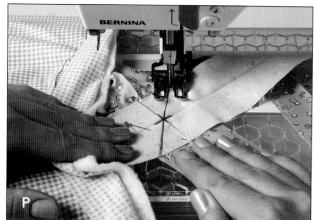

7. Lay binding against quilt to double-check that it is correct length (*Photo Q*). Trim ends of binding ¼" from diagonal seam (*Photo R*).

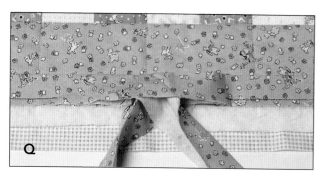

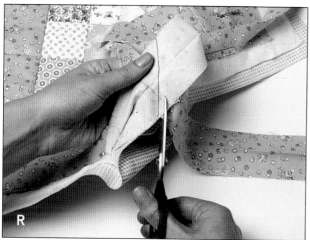

8. Finger press diagonal seam open (*Photo S*). Fold binding in half and finish stitching binding to quilt (*Photo T*).

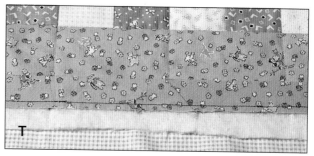

Hand Stitching Binding to Quilt Back

1. Trim any excess batting and quilt back with scissors or a rotary cutter (*Photo A*). Leave enough batting (about ⅛" beyond quilt top) to fill binding uniformly when it is turned to quilt back.

2. Bring folded edge of binding to quilt back so that it covers machine stitching. Blindstitch folded edge to quilt backing, using a few pins just ahead of stitching to hold binding in place (*Photo B*).

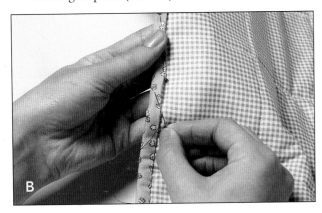

3. Continue stitching to corner. Fold unstitched binding from next side under, forming a 45-degree angle and a mitered corner. Stitch mitered folds on both front and back (*Photo C*).

Finishing Touches

● **Label your quilt so the recipient and future generations know who made it.** To make a label, use a fabric marking pen to write the details on a small piece of solid color fabric (*Photo A*). To make writing easier, put pieces of masking tape on the wrong side. Remove tape after writing. Use your iron to turn under ¼" on each edge, then stitch the label to the back of your quilt using a blindstitch, taking care not to sew through to quilt top.

● **Take a photo of your quilt.** Keep your photos in an album or journal along with notes, fabric swatches, and other information about the quilts.

● **If your quilt is a gift, include care instructions.** Some quilt shops carry pre-printed care labels you can sew onto the quilt (*Photo B*). Or, make a care label using the method described above.